Fascist Italy and Nazi Germany

'The book is perfectly pitched . . . It is an impressive and clear presentation of a very complex and central historical phenomenon . . . It offers a provocative and approachable thesis and argument for students to debate.'

Marla Stone, Occidental College

'An incredibly concise and manageable comparative analysis . . . Its combination of compression and comprehensiveness makes it ideal for students.'

Philip Morgan, University of Hull

Fascist Italy and Nazi Germany provides a succinct and provocative introduction to Italian fascism and German nazism. Incorporating recent historical research together with original and challenging arguments, Alexander J. De Grand examines:

* The similarities and differences in the early development of the two regimes
* The exercise of power by Adolf Hitler and Benito Mussolini
* The relationship between the two regimes
* Policies towards women, youth and culture.

Revised throughout, the second edition of this respected book takes account of recent historical research and includes an expanded discussion of the role of the military in the two regimes.

Alexander J. De Grand is Professor of Modern European History at North Carolina State University. He is the author of several books including *Italian Fascism: Its Origins and Development* (2000) and *In Stalin's Shadow: Angelo Tasca and the Crisis of the Left in Italy and France, 1910–1945* (1986).

Historical Connections

Series editors: Geoffrey Crossick, John Davis, Joanna Innes and Tom Scott

Fascist Italy and Nazi Germany

The 'fascist' style of rule

Second edition

Alexander J. De Grand

Routledge
Taylor & Francis Group

NEW YORK AND LONDON

First published 1995

Second edition published 2004
by Routledge
270 Madison Ave, New York, NY 10016

Simultaneously published in the UK
by Routledge
2 Park Square, Milton Park, Abingdon, Oxon OX14 4RN

© 1995, 2004 Alexander J. De Grand

Typeset in Times by
Florence Production Ltd, Stoodleigh, Devon
Printed and bound in Great Britain by
TJ International Ltd, Padstow, Cornwall

British Library Cataloguing in Publication Data
A catalogue record for this book is available from the British Library

Library of Congress Cataloging in Publication Data
A catalog record for this book has been applied for

ISBN 0–415–33629–5 (hbk)
ISBN 0–415–33631–7 (pbk)

Contents

Series editors' preface

Historical Connections is a series of short books on important historical topics and debates, written primarily for those studying and teaching history. The books will offer original and challenging works of synthesis that will make new themes accessible, or old themes accessible in new ways, build bridges between different chronological periods and different historical debates, and encourage comparative discussion in history.

If the study of history is to remain exciting and creative, then the tendency to fragmentation must be resisted. The inflexibility of older assumptions about the relationship between economic, social, cultural and political history has been exposed by recent historical writing, but the impression has sometimes been left that history is little more than a chapter of accidents. This series will insist on the importance of processes of historical change, and it will explore the connections within history: connections between different layers and forms of historical experience, as well as connections that resist the fragmentary consequences of new forms of specialism in historical research.

Historical Connections will put the search for these connections back at the top of the agenda by exploring new ways of uniting the different strands of historical experience, and by affirming the importance of studying change and movement in history.

Geoffrey Crossick
John Davis
Joanna Innes
Tom Scott

Acknowledgements

A number of friends and colleagues read various versions of the first edition: Joan Stewart, William Harris, Mary Ann Witt, Marion Miller, Anthony La Vopa, Philip Cannistraro, Walter Adamson, Alice Kelikian, Ruth Ben-Ghiat, Marla Stone, Spencer Di Scala and Donna Gabaccia. Their advice helped me avoid errors of fact and interpretation. Perhaps unwisely from his point of view, John Davis encouraged me to take on the project for the Historical Connections series. The Routledge editors, Claire L'Enfant and Heather McCallum (who has now moved on to other places) made working on the original edition a pleasure. Victoria Peters accepted my proposal for a new edition; Alex Ballantine worked with me with great patience and goodwill as I revised the manuscript. My Italian friends, Luigi and Caterina Lazzareschi and Luciana Capaccioli, provided advice and extended hospitality over many, many visits to the National Library in Florence. My debts to colleagues only grow for this new edition. Marla Stone, Marta Petrusewicz, Philip Morgan, Roger Griffin and Aristotle Kallis made suggestions on how I could improve the original edition. I tried to integrate their ideas into the new edition as far as possible. My e-mail friend, Robert Soucy, generously read the completed revision in record time and saved me from several inconsistencies. I am grateful to them all.

Chronology of the Fascist and Nazi regimes

29 July 1883 Birth of Benito Mussolini.

20 April 1889 Birth of Adolf Hitler.

June 1898–June 1900 Attempt to reverse parliamentary control and establish conservative executive government under General Luigi Pelloux.

1901 Giuseppe Zanardelli appointed Prime Minister with Giovanni Giolitti as Interior Minister. Era of liberal reform begins.

September 1903 Giovanni Giolitti appointed Prime Minister.

1907–1908 Italian economic crisis; slower growth from 1908–14.

September 1907 Hitler leaves Linz to go to Vienna.

1910 Foundation of the Italian Nationalist Association, right-wing authoritarian party, which will fuse with the Fascist Party in 1923.

September 1911 Italy goes to war with the Ottoman Empire over Libya.

1911 Benito Mussolini imprisoned for activities against war in Libya.

1912 Mussolini emerges as one of the leaders of the left wing of the Italian Socialist party at the Congress of Reggio Emilia; he is appointed editor of the party newspaper, *L'Avanti!*

1913 First Italian election under universal manhood suffrage law.

May 1913 Hitler moves from Vienna to Munich.

July 1914 Germany goes to war; Hitler enlists in German army in August.

October 1914 Benito Mussolini breaks with the Italian Socialist Party over continued Italian neutrality in First World War.

November 1914   Mussolini begins publication of his newspaper *Il Popolo d'Italia*, which will be published until the end of the regime.

May 1915   Italy enters First World War; Mussolini volunteers for service at the front.

October–November 1917   Italian defeat at Caporetto.

9 November 1918   Proclamation in Germany of the fall of the monarchy and the establishment of a republic.

11 November 1918   Germany signs armistice.

9 January 1919   Formation of the German Workers' Party by Anton Drexler in Munich.

19 January 1919   Election for the Constituent Assembly to draw up a constitution for the Weimar Republic; major victory for the German Social Democratic Party.

23 March 1919   Mussolini forms the first Fascio di Combattimento at Piazza San Sepoicro in Milan.

September 1919   Gabriele D'Annunzio seizes Fiume and holds it until December 1920 in defiance of Italian government; Hitler joins the German Workers' Party.

November 1919   Fascists badly defeated in national elections as Socialists and Catholics triumph.

13–17 March 1920   Kapp *putsch* against the Weimar Republic.

June 1920–July 1921   Giolitti's last government.

August–September 1920   Occupation of the automobile factories in Milan; climax of the agitation of the Red Years (1918–20).

August 1920   German Workers' Party transformed into the National Socialist German Workers' Party (NSDAP).

December 1920   D'Annunzio expelled from Fiume by Giolitti's government with Mussolini's backing.

May 1921   Mussolini included in Giolitti's National electoral list; the Fascists enter parliament with thirty-five deputies.

July 1921   Hitler becomes Chairman of the NSDAP; Giolitti government falls; Ivanoe Bonomi forms new government.

October 1921   Creation of the Sturmabteilung (SA), the Nazi paramilitary organization.

November 1921   Congress of the Fascist movement; creation of the National Fascist Party with a new conservative programme.

February 1922   Last weak liberal government under Luigi Facta formed.

27–9 October 1922 The March on Rome; Mussolini appointed Prime Minister.

November 1922 Mussolini government given exceptional decree law power by Parliament.

December 1922–January 1923 Fascist National Militia (MVSN) and the Fascist Grand Council created.

January–September 1923 Period in Germany of great inflation after the French occupy the industrial Ruhr area.

May 1923 New Fascist educational reform, drafted by Giovanni Gentile, passed.

November 1923 Acerbo electoral law passed: two-thirds of seats accorded to the list with the greatest number of votes.

8–9 November 1923 Nazi Beer Hall *putsch*; attempt to start the National Revolution against the Weimar Republic from Munich blocked by military.

11 November 1923 Hitler arrested after failed coup.

22 March 1924 Hitler given five-year sentence for participation in revolt.

April 1924 Victory for Fascists in national elections: 374 seats for Mussolini's National list, but Mussolini's ticket fails to carry major cities.

10 June 1924 Murder of Giacomo Matteotti; opposition withdraws from Parliament and appeals to king to remove Mussolini.

June 1924 Ex-Nationalist Luigi Federzoni made Minister of Interior.

December 1924 Hitler released after serving nine months of sentence; completed draft of Mein Kampf while in prison.

3 January 1925 Mussolini defies opposition to remove him; onset of the full dictatorship; decrees curbing the press put into effect.

January 1925 Alfredo Rocco made Justice Minister.

February 1925 Intransigent Fascist Roberto Farinacci made Fascist Party Secretary; NSDAP reorganized.

26 April 1925 Field Marshal Paul von Hindenburg elected President of the Weimar Republic.

1 May 1925 Creation of the Dopolavoro, the Fascist leisure-time organization for workers.

October 1925 Mussolini announces Battle for Grain.

2 October 1925   Palazzo Vidoni Accord; Italian Confederation of Industry agrees to grant the Fascist syndical confederation exclusive bargaining rights.

November–December 1925   Attempt on Mussolini's life by Socialist Tito Zaniboni; reformist Unitary Socialist Party outlawed, opposition press curbed; Law on the Powers of the Head of Government makes Mussolini responsible only to monarch.

March 1926   Farinacci replaced as PNF secretary by Augusto Turati.

April 1926   Rocco syndical law approved establishing one official labour and management organization in every section of the economy; official end of free trade union movement in Fascist Italy; creation of Fascist youth organization, Opera Nazionale Balilla.

July 1926   Creation of the Ministry of Corporations.

November–December 1926   Fascist Italy becomes a one-party state with the complete suppression of political opposition; expulsion and arrest of Communist deputies from parliament; legislation establishing category of political crimes against the regime and the creation of special courts; Luigi Federzoni replaced as Interior Minister by Mussolini.

April 1927   Charter of Labour issued.

May 1927   Mussolini's Ascension Day speech announces demographic campaign to increase birthrate.

1928   Breakup of the Fascist Syndical Confederation into six smaller units.

20 May 1928   National elections in Germany in which the NSDAP won twelve seats and 2.6 per cent of the vote but achieved significant gains in areas of peasant discontent in northern Germany; Socialist Heinrich Müller formed coalition government with Catholics and centre right parties.

February 1929   Lateran Treaty with the Catholic Church.

September 1929–July 1932   New Fascist government with Giuseppe Bottai as Minister of Corporations and Dino Grandi as Foreign Minister installed; debates over fascism as 'third way' between liberalism and bolshevism; debates over formation of the corporative system.

December 1929   Nazis make local breakthrough in state elections in Thuringia; Nazi Wilhelm Frick enters state government in early 1930.

29 March 1930 Müller government falls and Heinrich Brüning appointed Chancellor.

September 1930 Elections to the German Reichstag; NSDAP wins over 6 million votes or just over 18 per cent of total and 107 of 577 seats.

1931 Conflict between Fascist regime and Catholic Church over control of youth organizations.

August 1931 Imposition of loyalty oaths on professors and teachers; attempt to purge universities fails when only eleven professors refuse to take the oath.

September 1931 Agreement between the Fascist Party and Catholic Church over the role of Catholic youth groups.

November 1931 Creation of the Istituto Mobiliare Italiano to bail out banking system.

December 1931 Achille Starace appointed Secretary of the National Fascist Party; German unemployment reaches 5.6 million.

13 March 1932 Hitler receives 11.5 million votes in presidential election and forces Hindenburg into a run-off.

10 April 1932 Hitler receives over 13 million votes in losing runoff; Hindenburg re-elected.

30 May 1932 Brüning replaced as chancellor by Franz von Papen.

20 July 1932 Papen removes the Socialist-led government of Prussia, Germany's largest state.

31 July 1932 Elections to Reichstag; NSDAP wins 230 seats out of a total of 608 to become the largest parliamentary group. In the process, they take 37.4 per cent of the vote.

6 November 1932 Second Reichstag election; Nazi vote dropped to 11.7 million or 33 per cent and from 230 to 196 seats.

2 December 1932 Papen dismissed and General Kurt von Schleicher appointed Chancellor by President Hindenburg.

December 1932 Gregor Strasser loses battle for control of NSDAP to Hitler.

23 January 1933 Creation of the Istituto per la Riconstruzione Industriale (IRI); de facto nationalization of major industrial sectors begun as response to economic crisis.

30 January 1933 Adolf Hitler appointed Chancellor in a Hitler–Papen–Hugenberg government.

27 February 1933 Reichstag building destroyed by fire.

28 February 1933   Emergency decree suspends Weimar constitution.

March 1933   Coordination (Nazi takeover) of the state governments.

5 March 1933   Reichstag elections give Nazi Party 43.9 per cent of vote and 288 of 647 seats; German Nationalist allies win 52 seats.

13 March 1933   Josef Goebbels appointed as the head of the new Ministry for Popular Enlightenment and Propaganda.

23 March 1933   Passage of Enabling Act that gives the government decree power until 1937; marginalization of Parliament.

2 May 1933   Liquidation of the Socialist trade union movement.

6 May 1933   Creation of the German Labour Front (DAF) under Robert Ley.

19 May 1933   Law on Trustees of Labour; Nazi Germany ends collective bargaining.

8 July 1933   Concordat between the Vatican and the Nazi government signed.

14 July 1933   Law Against the Establishment of Political Parties passed; Germany officially becomes a one-party state.

22 September 1933   Goebbels creates the Reich Culture Chamber.

February 1934   Creation of the new system of Corporations.

June 1934   Hitler and Mussolini meet for first time in Venice.

30 June–2 July 1934   Purge of the SA; execution of Ernst Röhm and his close associates.

July 1934   Chancellor Engelbert Dollfuss of Austria is assassinated by Austrian Nazis; Mussolini mobilizes army on Brenner frontier with Austria; Conservative financier Hjalmar Schacht appointed as Minister of Economics in Hitler government.

2 August 1934   Hitler becomes Head of State and Chancellor on the death of Hindenburg.

December 1934   Incident between Ethiopian and Italian troops; opening of crisis leading to Italian conquest of Ethiopia.

February 1935   Mussolini appoints Felice Guarneri to head the Superintendency of Foreign Exchange; first moves towards autarky.

June 1935   Creation of the Ministry for Press and Propaganda under Galeazzo Ciano.

September 1935   Nuremberg Racial Laws; intensification of pressure on German Jewish community.

October 1935 Italy invades Ethiopia; sanctions imposed on Italy by the League of Nations.

December 1935 Creation of the Undersecretariat for Foreign Exchange; imposition of strict exchange controls over Italian industry and commerce.

March 1936 Autarky made official policy in Italy in response to League sanctions over Ethiopia; Hitler violates the demilitarized Rhineland; neither France nor Great Britain react.

June 1936 Mussolini names his son-in-law Galeazzo Giano as Foreign Minister; Hitler appoints Heinrich Himmler as Chief of German Police; consolidation of state and party security apparatus under Himmler.

September 1936 Göring put in charge of second Four Year Plan; Schacht and conservatives lose power struggle; Schacht will resign as Economics Minister in November 1937 and as Reichsbank President in January 1939.

October 1936 Creation of the Rome–Berlin Axis.

May 1937 Transformation of the Italian Ministry of Press and Propaganda into the Ministry for Popular Culture.

July 1937 Creation of the Reichswerke Hermann Göring; major step toward mobilization of economy for Nazi war policy.

October 1937 Consolidation of Fascist youth organizations under the umbrella of the Gioventù Italiana del Littorio (GIL) organization.

4 February 1938 Hitler dismisses War Minister von Blomberg and Army Chief von Fritsch to gain direct control of military; von Neurath is replaced by Ribbentrop at the Foreign Ministry.

March 1938 Austria annexed by Germany.

July 1938 Initiation of the anti-Semitic campaign in Italy.

12–30 September 1938 Crisis over Czechoslovakia resolved with partition of the Czech Republic at Munich Conference on 30 September.

9–10 November 1938 Kristallnacht pogrom against German Jewish businesses and synagogues.

February 1939 Fascist School Charter.

March 1939 Chamber of Fasci and Corporations replaces the old Italian Chamber of Deputies.

15 March 1939 Germany seizes Prague and absorbs Czech Republic.

22 May 1939   Pact of Steel alliance between Nazi Germany and Fascist Italy signed.

23 August 1939   Ribbentrop–Molotov pact between Nazi Germany and USSR at the expense of Poland.

1–3 September 1939   Invasion of Poland by Germany; Great Britain and France declare war on Germany; Italy remains neutral at outbreak of Second World War.

March 1940   Hitler and Mussolini meet; Italian entry into war promised.

10 May 1940   German invasion of Holland, Belgium and France begun.

10 June 1940   Italy declares war on France.

17 June 1940   France calls for armistice.

October 1940–early 1941   Italy attacks Greece and is badly defeated; end of the Fascist 'parallel war' strategy.

December 1940–February 1941   Collapse of Italian position in North Africa.

April 1941   Germany attacks Yugoslavia and Greece to reverse Italian humiliation.

22 June 1941   Germany attacks the USSR; Italy joins war against the USSR.

January 1942   Wannsee Conference at which the Final Solution to the Jewish problem was discussed but policy set somewhat earlier.

January 1943   German Army surrenders at Stalingrad.

February 1943   Reshuffling of Italian government; Ciano ousted as Foreign Minister.

24–5 July 1943   Fascist Grand Council rejects Mussolini's leadership; King Victor Emmanuel removes Mussolini and appoints Marshal Pietro Badoglio as Prime Minister.

8 September 1943   Italy accepts armistice with the Allies; Germany occupies the peninsula.

12–13 September 1943   Mussolini rescued from prison by German aviators and brought to Germany.

14–15 September 1943   Proclamation of the Italian Social Republic in the German-controlled part of Italy.

20 July 1944   Failure of military attempt on life of Hitler.

26–8 April 1945   Arrest and execution of Mussolini by Italian partisans.

30 April 1945   Suicide of Hitler in Berlin.

Introduction

When I began work on the first edition of this book, efforts to find a framework within which various fascist movements and regimes could be understood was just beginning after a hiatus of over a decade. During the 1980s scholars had more or less given up trying to find a Fascist minimum and had begun to treat Italy and Germany as distinctly separate regimes. Most of the work on Fascist Italy and on Nazi Germany was not comparative in the 1980s and early 1990s. Since the publication of the first edition of this book, three new directions have opened up. First, comparative studies of Fascist Italy and Nazi Germany have become much more common, although the connections have been made more on the level of ideology than in methods of governing, which is the subject of this study.[1] Second, the debate on generic fascism and the fascist minimum has taken on new life with the publication of works by Roger Griffin, Stanley Payne, Roger Eatwell and Robert Paxton.[2] Finally, the concept of totalitarianism, which had fallen into disuse with the waning of the Cold War, was re-evaluated as a tool for looking at the fascist experience. One of the objections to the earlier use of the term was that it seemed to leave out Italy, while linking Hitler's Germany and Stalin's Soviet Union. Although this approach offered some satisfaction to Cold Warriors who favoured lumping the USSR with the despised Nazi state, it was conceptually unsatisfying to leave out the Italian regime that gave fascism its name. The new version of totalitarian theory is less willing to leave Italy outside, even if the Italian totalitarian project remained largely on paper.[3]

This account builds on the recent work on German and Italian fascism. It assumes that the two regimes have much in common.

The initial movements arose, almost simultaneously, out of the crisis of post-First World War Europe. A great part of pre-fascist society was carried over into the regimes and the same social order largely survived the fall of fascism and nazism. That this was so might be considered strange, since both regimes claimed to have created revolutionary new societies.

As in the first edition, I would like to concentrate on connections and differences between the two regimes that arose out of practice from 1919 to the outbreak of the Second World War. Given the limitations of space and the rapid decline of Italian fascism after 1940, events during the Second World War still receive only a brief glance. However, more attention must be paid to the research that has recently been published on generic fascist ideology and to the major new works on Hitler and Mussolini.[4] Clearly, the Duce and the Führer differed in many ways, but they shared a common view of politics as violent struggle in which only the strong would survive. Survival was intrinsically connected in their minds to expansion. Thus, war was central to their ideology. Neither Mussolini nor Hitler accepted any distinction between domestic and foreign policy. The former provided the means by which the latter would succeed and success abroad would ensure the expansion and health of the nation or race. Neither man could live within the status quo; therefore, neither could create a stable system of power. Mussolini came closest, but in the end he deliberately destabilized his own political system after 1935.

Both regimes proposed powerful national or racial myths that contained equally strong positive and negative messages. In the Nazi and Fascist world view, the people or the race were threatened by powerful internal and foreign enemies. These incompatible elements first had to be excluded from the national community and then defeated abroad. Both Hitler and Mussolini aimed at re-educating their respective societies according to an entirely new set of values that would be a repudiation of the humanitarian and rationalist tradition of the Enlightenment in both its liberal and socialist form. Nowhere is this rupture more apparent than on the issues of creating a new community and racial policy. Since completing the first edition, I have come to believe that the divergence between fascism and nazism on racial policy is not as great as I believed. Both regimes used race partly as an instrument in the realization of a totalitarian state. If this is true, then Italian

Fascist racial policies during the late 1930s were not an aberration or an attempt to align Italy with Nazi Germany, but a logical extension of the essential nature of the regime.

Significant parallels between the regimes can also be seen in two areas: first, in the origins and early development of the movements and their rise to power; second, and more importantly, in their approach to organizing the state once power had been achieved. The Fascist and Nazi regimes were confronted by a double problem. Despite the presence of some working-class and peasant support, their primary social base was in the middle class. This fact limited the potential rupture with the existing society, with its administrative elites and with the structure of private capital. The fact that the core groups of both movements were composed of outsiders and predominantly young, impatient veterans only increased the tension with the established order.[5] Inevitably, a distinctive power-sharing arrangement developed even before the Fascists or Nazis formed their governments. But these compromises were fraught with substantial tension between parts of the 'fascist' coalition. In the search for some common denominator that could hold the alliance together and bring it to power, both movements were forced, even before entering the government, to jettison their radical programmes for a fundamental restructuring of social and economic institutions. The new conception of the national or racial community was compromised from the start. What resulted was the fragmentation of the state into semi-autonomous power centres under highly personalized dictatorships that embodied in the person of the supreme leader the unity that had not been realized in practice. Any attempt to construct a common framework for fascism and nazism must start with an analysis of this attempt to forge symbolic unity within a system of government that was *by nature* fragmented and inchoate.[6]

1 Fascism and nazism before the seizure of power

Fascism in Italy, Germany and elsewhere in western Europe was a response to certain problems inherent in the structure of liberal politics around the turn of the century: the adoption of universal suffrage, the crisis of nineteenth-century bourgeois political organizations, the development of socialist parties and trade unions and a growing impatience on the part of industrial and agrarian elites with the inadequacies of the existing parliamentary system. The First World War increased generational conflicts within the middle class, ideological polarization over the issue of the war and over the Bolshevik Revolution and rising expectations among all classes that fed both revolutionary and counter-revolutionary aspirations. But it would be wrong to see 'fascism' as merely a defensive manoeuvre on the part of a desperate and reactionary bourgeoisie to ward off inevitable revolution. The Fascist and Nazi movements were expressions of the expansion of the bourgeoisie and its desire to see society organized in ways that favoured its continued social ascent.

General conditions provided opportunities, nothing more. But two things were central to the destabilization of the nineteenth-century political and social order. The emergence of the Socialist movement and institutionalized trade union activity increased the pressure to redistribute political power and to include new groups in the social and economic balance. In Italy and Germany these demands were rejected by large sectors of the middle class. Moreover, existing bourgeois political organizations proved themselves unable to reassure their constituencies that they could deal with the competition of mass politics. Parliamentary institutions in both countries had been found wanting even before the war.

A dangerous split developed between bourgeois political parties and the wide variety of social and economic groups that existed and increased in number, especially in Wilhelmine and Weimar Germany, before the rise of fascism and nazism. The gap between the political and the social, cultural and economic organizations of the bourgeoisie created its own pressure for a resolution in a national middle-class political movement.

The timing was roughly similar in Italy and Germany. The Italian crisis began when the economic crisis of 1907–8 reduced the manoeuvring room for the reformist strategy designed by the great liberal leader, Giovanni Giolitti, accelerated with the Libyan war of 1911–12, the introduction of universal male suffrage for the elections of 1913 and the outbreak of the First World War and concluded in the radicalized political climate of the postwar era. The German elections of 1912 in which the Social Democratic Party (SPD) emerged totally isolated as the largest political party could be said to have marked the beginning of the crisis that continued through the war and then played itself out in the Weimar Republic.

The most sustained attempt to broaden the basis of the Italian liberal parliamentary state came under Giovanni Giolitti from 1901 to 1914. When Giolitti inaugurated his policy of toleration of working-class organizations in 1901, he did so under exceptionally favourable circumstances. Italy had begun a growth spurt in the late 1890s that lasted until the depression of 1907–8. The government took advantage of favourable interest rates to refinance its public debt.[1] These windfall profits allowed freer collective bargaining in the private sector and some increased social benefits, along with traditionally heavy military outlays. The margins for expansion were not great. Agrarian strikes in 1901 and 1902 produced wage concesions favourable to the peasant unions, but the government and the landowners took a much harder line after 1903. During the ten years before the First World War, cooperation among the liberal political establishment, the unions and the socialist party waxed and waned but never took on durable institutional form. After 1908, as economic growth slowed, social tensions rose. The longtime political leader Giovanni Giolitti returned to office in 1911 on a programme that included universal manhood suffrage. Inevitably, the first elections held in 1913 under the new system marked the decline of liberal hegemony in Italy.

One need not enter the *Sonderweg* debates over just how far the Bismarckian and Wilhelmine parliamentary state differed from the norm of western European bourgeois liberalism to realize that Germany's political system also faced serious problems shortly before the First World War. In the elections of 1912 the German Social Democratic Party polled well over 4 million votes in the first round of balloting and received 110 of 390 seats in the new Reichstag, but the largest parliamentary party was completely without allies. The 1912 elections were conducted against the Socialists by competing bourgeois alliances. The great Socialist victory put the moderate middle-class parties – the Progressives and the National Liberals – in a quandary. Antiquated features in the political system, such as the three-class voting system in Prussia and the rural bias in Reichstag voting, blocked reform. Although Imperial Germany had competitive elections with universal manhood suffrage for the national Reichstag, the full impact of democratic politics was muted by the quite different rules that governed local elections in many German states and the constitutional limitations on parliamentary control of the national government and even on the participation of parties *per se* in the imperial ministries. Germany's well-organized economic elites – the Centralverband Deutscher Industrieller for heavy industry, the Bund der Industriellen for light and export-oriented industry, the Chambers of Commerce, the groups representing the military–industrial alliance like the Navy League and the Army League, individual production cartels and the Bund der Landwirte (Agrarian League) – were built into the governmental structures on the highest levels and had their parliamentary interests protected by the Conservative and the National Liberal Parties. Change demanded an alliance with the Social Democratic Party that middle-class voters were unlikely to support. The Socialist vote revealed growing discontent with the existing system but offered no solutions. In fact, it provoked a counter-movement to reinforce executive power and modify the system of universal manhood suffrage for imperial elections.

The outbreak of the First World War accelerated the decomposition of the middle-class political order in both states. Italian national unity was in question from the very outset of the conflict. A governmental crisis in March 1914 brought to power the conservative Antonio Salandra as head of a Ministry of Bourgeois Concentration. Although the ministry opted for neutrality in August

1914, the decision to intervene on the side of the Entente in May 1915 was made against the will of Giolitti who still commanded a sizeable following in parliament, and virtually brought to a halt any restructuring of middle-class party organizations. Wartime cabinets rested on an extremely fragile consensus. Only victory and full realization of Italy's war aims could have saved its leaders from answering for the terrible losses caused by the war.

Three events in 1917 marked the crisis in Italian political life. During the summer, widespread strikes, notably in Turin, revealed growing worker discontent over rising prices and food shortages. News of the Bolshevik Revolution in October added an emotional issue powerful enough to push the Italian Socialist Party further to the left. Finally, Italy's defeat at Caporetto at the end of October considerably raised the stakes of the war for the governing class.

From November 1918 to October 1922 the latent problems of the political system came to the fore. Just as before the war, no framework for interclass cooperation could be established, nor could the new parliament reconcile competing interests. One hundred and fifty-six Socialist deputies, most of whom were convinced of the possibility of a Bolshevik-style revolution in Italy and were determined to block any reformist solution to the crisis, entered the Chamber of Deputies in 1919. The marginalization of its largest party inevitably weakened parliament. The two progressive governments, headed successively by Francesco Nitti and Giovanni Giolitti from June 1919 to July 1921, were unable to find common ground between industrial management and landowners on one side and the trade unions and peasant leagues on the other. Gains made in the initial strike wave of 1919 were lost by demobilization and the transition to a peace economy and by growing resistance to worker demands in 1920.[2]

Defeat in the First World War altered even more drastically the basis of German postwar politics. First, by destroying the old political system, the war threw into question the relations between industry, the bureaucracy and the executive power. By the end of the war, long-established arrangements were in shambles. Moreover, the onset of the war in 1914 had begun a period of economic crisis for Germany that lasted throughout much of the interwar period. After decades of steady growth from the 1880s to the outbreak of the war, the economic instability of the 1920s and early 1930s exacerbated the crisis in political relationships caused by the creation of the Weimar Republic. Finally, the war aggravated a generational crisis that had been brewing even before 1914. By the mid-1920s the number of young people aged between 15 and 25 peaked, just when the labour market was least able to absorb these young workers. By 1932, one-quarter of the unemployed were aged between 14 and 25 years. Not only did the trench generation emerge from the war disoriented and embittered, but the generation that followed fared no better.[3]

The Bolshevik Revolution and the failed German revolution of 1918 compromised the birth of the Weimar Republic and weakened the SPD, its largest political party. Nonetheless, during the brief life of Germany's democratic experience, the SPD played a key role. No two parties could have been more dissimilar than the chaotic and badly organized Italian Socialist Party and the highly disciplined and wealthy German Social Democratic Party, yet their fate was much the same. The Italian party, dominated by its revolutionary or maximalist wing, refused to participate in bourgeois governments and remained passive during the crisis of the liberal parliamentary system. The German Social Democratic party was controlled by its reformist wing, although it was under pressure from a growing Communist left. The SPD had been a party of government from late 1918 until 1920 and again from 1928 to March 1930 and controlled the Prussian government, almost always in alliance with the Centre party, until 1932.

However, neither party had been fully integrated into the system of parliamentary politics. True, the bulk of Italian socialists, blinded by an almost mystical faith in revolutionary possibilities, excluded themselves. But there is no doubt that once it became clear that even the reformist socialists might be dispensed with, most bourgeois politicians did so without a second thought. The German Socialists managed to entrench themselves in the bureaucracy of the Labour Ministry in order to protect their working-class constituents against the erosion of union bargaining power. However, they found that, with the onset of the depression, the aims of most industrialists and of the conservative politicians were so at odds with labour that continued cooperation in the government meant total acquiescence on the part of the Socialists to cuts in social benefits and to forced wage reductions. Once the votes of the SPD – the largest parliamentary bloc after the 1928 elections

– were eliminated, the bourgeois parties had to govern alone. Chancellor Heinrich Brüning's ill-advised decision to call elections in September 1930 made the political situation well-nigh impossible. His idea, like Giolitti's before him, was to punish the SPD and diminish its influence. Instead, he allowed the Nazis to increase their seats from twelve to over a hundred.[4]

2 The rise of fascism and nazism

Fascism and nazism appeared in 1919 as movements that brought together diverse groups of political and cultural dissidents without imposing a high degree of party discipline or a demand of exclusive membership. Only at a second stage – after 1921 for the National Fascist Party (PNF) and after 1925 for the National Socialist Workers' Party (NSDAP) – did the movements become true parties. The outsiders constituting the Fascist and Nazi movements shared many values. Above all, they were alienated from the direction that modern industrial culture was taking at the end of the nineteenth century. They believed (quite clearly in the case of the Italian Futurists) that different conclusions from those of progressive democrats and socialists might be drawn without completely rejecting industrial society. Their views were expressed as a radical repudiation of the liberal and parliamentary political order that took the form of anti-materialism and the search for new spiritual values, anti-socialism, appreciation of the irrational forces in modern society and glorification of instinct and violence in political life.[1]

The coalition of dissidents behind Italian fascism had certain distinctive characteristics that set it apart from the Nazi cultural fringe. As both Zeev Sternhell and Walter Adamson persuasively argue, it was rooted more in Franco-Italian intellectual traditions, a fact that led Mussolini and many of his colleagues to view the war against Germany as a sort of cultural crusade. Leftist and reactionary traditions were deliberately blended in Italian fascism, as might be expected in a movement that was evolving rightward but had been founded by ex-socialists and syndicalists. Certainly, little mysticism or anti-Semitism was present, although nothing in the Fascist ideology precluded an evolution towards anti-Semitism.[2]

In 1919, however, the Fascist movement was far from becoming the preferred instrument of social restoration. Mussolini's first Fascio di Combattimento, which met in Milan on 23 March 1919, was, even more than the initial National Socialist movement, a great failure. No political space existed for a nationalist alternative on the left. Like Mussolini himself, many initial recruits came from the socialist or syndicalist movement and had been converted to nationalism during the campaign for Italian intervention in the First World War. On 1 August 1918, Mussolini altered the masthead of his newspaper, *Il Popolo d'Italia*, from 'socialist daily' to 'daily of the fighters and producers'. The change ratified his conversion to 'productivism', a doctrine put forward simultaneously on the extreme right by the nationalist writer, Enrico Corradini. Class was no longer the dividing line for political action. The fundamental rift was not between bourgeois and proletarian Italy or between capitalists and workers, but between the productive forces on the battlefields and in the factories and the unproductive exploiters – politicians, war profiteers and anti-war socialists. Mussolini's productivism united FIAT's Giovanni Agnelli with the ordinary car worker and military Commander-in-Chief Armando Diaz with the infantryman. This corporative ideology of interclass cooperation had little appeal to workers in the polarized political atmosphere of 1918 and 1919.[3]

Veterans and students, attracted by nationalism and activism, joined the Fascio di Combattimento and the Nazi movement in 1919 and 1920. While not out of place in 1919, the early radical programme had been a tactic in the war against the existing political class and could be abandoned or ignored. The Fascists never gave priority to systematic changes in the social and economic structure of Italy anyway. Their target was the Italian political class. They wanted a social system that rewarded *competenze*, merit won on the battlefield or in the classroom.

The history of the NSDAP before the seizure of power can be divided into three periods: from the founding of the party in 1919 to the Beer Hall *putsch* of 8–9 November 1923; from 1925 to the great electoral victory of September 1930; and from late 1930 to Hitler's appointment as Chancellor on 30 January 1933. The first and part of the second period until 1928 roughly paralleled the Fascist movement's development from March 1919 until the PNF congress of autumn 1921. Like the Fascists, the Nazis gradually abandoned or ignored parts of their old programme. The NSDAP also shifted from an urban strategy that directly challenged the Socialists and Communists for control of the working class to one that focused on peasants and various middle-class constituencies. Here again, the Nazis paralleled the development of the Fascist Party in 1921 and 1922. However, the nature of this rural support was significantly different. The Nazis did not need (nor did it exist) a socialist challenge on the land because the SPD had no comparable organization to the Italian Socialist peasant leagues. Certainly, anti-socialism and especially anti-communism played a large role in Nazi success as well, but it was outweighed by general anger among small peasant holders arising from the agricultural depression of 1927. The NSDAP exploited the bitterness of the small farming peasant and the artisans against the 'middlemen' who were equated with Jews. A comparable attack would not have worked in Italy where the presence of large-scale retailing was less developed and where the Italian Jews had never occupied a significant role in the rural economy. For the Fascists, the enemy was the 'left', whether Socialist, Communist or Catholic, but defined in political rather than racial terms, anti-Slav feelings in the north-eastern part of Italy notwithstanding.

The German Workers' Party that Anton Drexler, a toolmaker for the Bavarian railways in Munich, founded on 9 January 1919, bore some initial similarities to the first *fascio* that Mussolini formed two months later in Milan. Both movements sought to carve out political space on the nationalist and populist left. Their programme of radical economic and social reforms avoided the issue of class conflict by injecting all points with a dose of nationalism. Mussolini used 'productivism' to bridge the lines of class conflict; Drexler and his recruit Adolf Hitler, who joined the German Workers' Party in September 1919, combined anti-Semitism with populist attacks on 'finance capital' and calls for profit sharing. Gottfried Feder, an engineer and self-taught economic expert, developed the economic agenda of the new movement. Like the first Fascist programme, these aspects of the Nazi platform appealed mainly to artisans and self-employed workers who were in fact somewhat over-represented in the movement. In the political climate of 1919 it had little attraction for industrial workers and alienated middle-class and industrialist support. By 1920 the movement, renamed the National Socialist German

Workers' Party, found what would become its social centre of gravity. The new programme of 1920 directly appealed to the lower middle class by combining anti-Semitism with hostility to large commercial enterprises, attacks on cooperatives and hostility to immigration.[4]

The Nazi movement also blended traditional *völkisch* and nationalist thought with its shadings of cultural pessimism, virulent racial ideologies and the fanatical 'steel romanticism' of the 'trench generation', expressed in the Freikorps and subsequently the SA. Men like Rudolf Hess and Gottfried Feder through their common membership in organizations such as the Thule Society linked the new Nazi movement to the *völkisch* and racist right, and racial utopian organizations like the Artaman League brought Heinrich Himmier together with future Auschwitz Commandant Rudolf Höss.

Nationalism, male bonding and anti-socialist activism played a role in drawing Italian veterans and German ex-Freikorps members into the movements. The core of both movements was this front generation, born in the 1890s and, for the Nazis, the disillusioned generation that came of age in the 1920s: Strasser, Ernst Röhm, Göring, Hess and Hitler belong to the trench generation; Martin Bormann and Heinrich Himmier, both born in 1900, came of age in the turbulent Weimar years. The Fascist elite was largely from the 1880 to 1895 period. Italo Balbo, Dino Grandi, Giuseppe Bottai and Mussolini himself were in their late twenties and thirties at the time of the March on Rome in October 1922.[5]

3   The march to power

Like the Nazi seizure of power ten years later, the Fascist March on Rome encompassed two parallel movements. In the country the Fascists conducted a systematic, often province-wide campaign of direct action in 1921 and 1922. But such violence, even when successful, could never ensure power. If the aim had merely been to defeat an already prostrate left, neither the Fascist nor Nazi movements would have been included in the government. Clearly, other interests had to come into play. No doubt the considerable base in the country that had been built up by both movements was vital, but alone it was insufficient. The Fascists, in particular, were still a relatively small parliamentary grouping of thirty-five deputies after the 1921 elections.

The Fascists and Nazis came to power because of deep divisions within the political elite and a desire on the part of important economic and social interests to escape from the prolonged political crisis. The constitutional and structural defects of the Weimar Republic that facilitated Hitler's rise are well known. Proportional representation in Germany increased the power of party bureaucracies and caused a fragmentation of the electorate, while at the same time rendering politics more remote and abstract in the eyes of both Italian and German voters, The famous Article 48 on presidential emergency powers allowed power to fall into the hands of a few advisers to President von Hindenburg, just as the Italian constitution left key decisions to the king about whom to appoint to form a government.

The crisis that led to the appointment of Mussolini and Hitler had two dimensions. The first resulted from the determination of conservatives to eliminate the left, which had controlled a large part

of parliament and had institutionalized its power through recognition of union bargaining rights and other concessions won during
the immediate postwar years. In both pre-fascist Italy and Weimar
Germany the socialists had been defeated by a combination of legal
and extra-constitutional mechanisms, but their *potential* for recovery remained. By late 1920 landowners in northern and central Italy
were determined to break permanently the power of the peasant
leagues, the rural cooperatives and socialist control over local government. In 1921 and 1922, they feared that the socialist left and
the small but growing Communist Party might recover if the
pressure were removed. In Weimar Germany the Communist Party
was expanding in 1932 almost as rapidly as the Nazi movement.
Moreover, even the efforts of the most moderate socialists to
protect welfare benefits for workers interfered with the desire of
employers to cut wages and taxation. This first problem was intrinsically connected to the second – the crisis of the political class.
Because the traditional bourgeois parties had not succeeded in
winning a mass electorate, all the leaders vying for power in Italy
– former prime ministers Giovanni Giolitti, Antonio Salandra,
Vittorio Emanuele Orlando, Francesco Nitti – attempted to co-opt
the Fascist mass organization in order to create a stable political
majority. Although Mussolini's Fascists directly controlled only
thirty-five votes in parliament, their presence ensured the possibility of order in the country at large. Rivalries between the leading
political figures made Mussolini and Hitler the least objectionable
choices in the eyes of many conservatives.

Ideology played a limited part in the decision of the political
leadership and economic elites to accept the Fascists and Nazis.
The Fascists really had no clear ideology before taking power,
except a commitment to strong government and charismatic leadership. Anti-socialism and nationalism were sufficient program-
matic positions; for the rest, the Fascists assured the conservatives
that nothing drastic would be attempted in the economic and social
areas. Historians disagree about how much of the radical 'fascism
of the first hour' survived from 1921 to 1943, but there is no doubt
that the Fascist movement shifted gear in 1921.[1] These changes
were symbolized in the moderate economic and social programme
of the Partito Nazionale Fascista (PNF) that emerged from the
Fascist Congress in November 1921. Nor did the Fascists know

what they wanted to do after 29 October 1922. Mussolini and his colleagues improvised as they went along and made a virtue of the fact. Just as surely, the Nazis did not come to power because they were anti-Semitic or because they emphasized the economic ideas of the more fanatic representatives of the Nazi *Mittelstand* organizations. More than a well-defined political entity, 'fascism' in the broadest sense was a process in continuous development and transformation.

The true structure of the Fascist movement in 1921 and 1922 was at the provincial level where, during the two years preceding the March on Rome, the blackshirts engaged in the systematic dismantling of Socialist and union power. Local chieftans or *ras* launched punitive expeditions against the socialists and left-wing Catholics, often in alliance with local landlords, businessmen and military commanders. While the socialist revolutionaries of 1919 directed a largely verbal assault upon representatives of the basic institutions of the state, the Fascists assured these same targets of abuse agrarian and industrial leaders, the Church, and the army that the PNF had no intention of changing anything but the distribution of authority within the political class.

Before the seizure of power some Fascists were republicans, as Mussolini had been until 1921; others supported the monarchy. A few vaunted their social and economic radicalism, while the majority were evolving to positions more acceptable to the existing establishment. All shared a belief that liberal individualism had allowed society to fragment and had opened the door to class warfare.

The Fascists did have a distinct social base, however. In those provinces with strong Socialist organizations, the Fascist counter-revolution was particularly vigorous (with the exception of Giolitti's Piedmont). The Fascist push was strongest in the northern provinces of Emilia, Lombardy, Tuscany and the Veneto and much weaker in the South and on the islands. The middle and lower middle class was over-represented in the Fascist Party in 1921, while workers comprised 15.5 per cent of members and peasants 24.3 per cent. This latter figure indicates the desperation of peasants to seek protection in the new Fascist peasant leagues after the destruction of their socialist organizations, but rural fascism also drew smaller landowners and leaseholders who resented the domination of the Socialist leagues. Students and the new provincial

professional and bureaucratic middle class were also well represented.[2] This disparate middle-class coalition was united by
common nationalism, determination to crush the Socialists and
ambitions to supplant the existing political class on the local and
national level. A mystique grew up around the punitive expeditions of the squads and the comradeship in struggle against the
socialists (as well as on the disputed borderlands against the Slavic
minorities). The emotions of the trenches were projected into
postwar political battles.[3] The Nazis recreated the same mentality
in the provincial, lower middle-class and working-class National
Socialism of the SA. This violent and undisciplined fraternity was
the strength of the Fascist and Nazi movements on their way to
power, but it would be a major problem for the leadership once
power was achieved and the expectations of the spoils of victory
were inevitably disappointed.[4]

Nazi participation in the disastrous *coup* attempt of 8–9
November 1923 marked the demise of the original movement.
When the NSDAP resurfaced in 1925, its activities were charac-
terized by several new elements. While remaining strong in
Bavaria, the NSDAP shifted a major organizational effort north-
ward thanks to the work of the energetic Gregor Strasser and Josef
Goebbels. The Nazi movement became a true national party,
although its urban strategy failed and the NSDAP only stumbled
on the rich vein of rural protest votes in 1928.

The failure of the appeal to workers from 1926 to 1928
was attributable in part to Hitler's refusal to sanction an official
Nazi trade union movement. In *Mein Kampf* the Führer clearly
stated that

> it is dangerous to link an ideological struggle too soon to mat-
> ters of economics. This could easily lead to economic aspects
> directing the political movement instead of the ideology forc-
> ing the trade unions into its course . . . A Nationalist socialist
> trade union which sees its mission only in competition with the
> Marxists would be worse than none.[5]

Mussolini took a similar position for somewhat different
reasons. As an ex-socialist, the future Duce did not want to fore-
close an opening to part of the reformist Socialist union movement.
Thus he kept Edmondo Rossoni's syndical movement at arm's

length, while allowing the formation of Fascist peasant leagues on a provincial basis. In the Nazi movement, Strasser, not Hitler, adopted the strategy of labour alliances. Hitler, with no socialist past, had little interest in the development of a powerful Nazi left wing that might be used by Strasser as a basis for a future leadership challenge. Like Mussolini, Hitler allowed the formation of a peasant organization and a small Nazi Factory Cell Organization (NSBO). Whatever the motives, the decision to exclude a large organized worker presence de-emphasized the proletarian component of both movements and facilitated an understanding with industrialists and agrarians. Even before taking power. Fascists and Nazis grasped that their mission was to cut the Marxist-dominated unions from the worker-management equation.

Some latitude was given to provincial Nazi leaders to experiment with local issues provided that the authority of Hitler was recognized. One of the characteristic features of Nazi rule emerged almost from the beginning. This was the pull between imposing a rational, centralized organization on the NSDAP and *ad hoc* organizational practice at the Länder level. After 1926 the party's central office, the Reichsleitung, exercised increasing financial control over local organizations, but these formal controls only went so far. The Gauleiters were appointed personally by Hitler and could be removed by him. A local leader who enjoyed Hitler's absolute trust and favour had a high degree of independence. Until the very end of the regime a long-standing Gauleiter could always trump efforts to rein him in by a personal appeal to Hitler.

Before the seizure of power, the central party leadership's own need for funds imposed constant burdens on Gau district branches. In this regard, the Nazi movement paralleled the earlier growth of the Fascist Party, at least until Mussolini became Prime Minister in October 1922. But the Nazis' prolonged drive to power created the need for a more elaborate organizational apparatus than was demanded from the Fascists, who only competed in one election (April 1921) before coming to power. The Nazis had to organize for constant and costly electioneering on the state and national level from 1928 to 1932.

The elections of 1928 gave the illusion of stability to the Weimar Republic. The combined Socialist (29.8 per cent) and Communist (10.7 per cent) vote reached about 40 per cent of the electorate but, of course, it was a vote that could never be combined because of the deep hostility between the two parties after 1918. All the potential allies of the SPD in the political centre lost ground. The Nazis received only 2.6 per cent of the vote nationally but managed a substantial breakthrough in Schleswig-Holstein, Lower Saxony, Thuringia and Upper Bavaria where the movement took advantage of the agricultural depression and peasant hostility to all established parties. Although the main rightist party, the anti-Semitic reactionary National Peoples Party (DNVP) dropped from 20 per cent to 14.3 per cent of the vote in the elections of 1924, the extreme right stabilized at 30 per cent of the electorate during the most prosperous Weimar years.[6] The SPD-Centre (Catholic)-DDP–DVP coalition had about 58 per cent of the vote, but the right wing of that coalition, the Democratic Party (DDP) (5 per cent) and the German People's Party (DVP) (8.6 per cent), had been steadily declining in voter favour.

The challenge for the NSDAP, as it had been for the PNF, was to unify the rural and urban bourgeois bloc. Both Mussolini and Hitler competed with bourgeois rivals who appealed to particular local or class interests but who could not mobilize broader middle-class aspirations for a global solution to the political crisis. They were also confronted by a Catholic party whose control over its electorate could not be broken but only neutralized. Mussolini cultivated the right wing of the Catholic Italian Popular Party, just as Hitler worked on Franz von Papen who nominally belonged to the German Centre party. These initial manoeuvres paved the way for rupturing Catholic unity once the two movements arrived in power. But with the bulk of the Catholic vote out of reach, both movements worked on the amorphous, generically conservative vote. In Italy this tactic meant an appeal to the frightened and angry moderate voters; in Germany it meant winning over the Protestant middle class.

The Fascists and Nazis relied on local successes to create a sense of inevitability that propelled them to power. The Fascists, buoyed up by their initial successful assault on the peasant leagues in Emilia and Ferrara, rapidly gained adherents throughout the entire Po Valley. They turned a revolt of the provincial middle class into the drive for power at the national level. The Nazis led a similar revolt of the provincial middle classes of Germany against leaders and parties that represented narrow interests but could not present a vision of a unified society. In 1928 they swept aside older provincial elites such as the DNVP and Landwirte leaders in Schleswig-Holstein by winning as much as 18 per cent of the vote in some parts of Schleswig-Holstein, well above their national average. In 1929 the NSDAP won an absolute majority in the city of Coburg in northern, Protestant Franconia followed by a victory in state elections in Thuringia that allowed Hitler to install Wilhelm Frick as Thuringian Interior Minister in early 1930.

Although the Nazis varied their appeal from place to place, they knitted it together with a vision of a *Volksgemeinschaft*, or 'people's community'. Large numbers of young people, just coming of age at the time of the Great Depression, found this stress on solidarity attractive.[7] Although both Nazis and Communists profited from this unsettled youth vote, the former belonged to the only middle-class party that could compete for it nationally after 1930. Forty per cent of the new members were under 30 years of age.[8] They made their presence felt in all areas through their soup kitchens for the unemployed, the confrontational tactics of the brownshirts and unceasing propaganda against those in power.

The amazing success of both the Fascists and the Nazis inevitably raises the issue of finances. How did they pay for their assault on power and what was their relationship to the major industrial and agrarian 'deep pockets'? The Fascists exploded on to the political scene as a fighting force, closely tied to provincial agrarian and agrobusiness interests. Fascist gangs carried out their punitive expeditions on trucks donated by local landowners and military authorities. Compared to the Nazis who ran a large-scale mass party largely through dues, sale of party materials and donations from small and medium-sized business groups, the Fascists operated in a more rudimentary fashion until they took power.[9]

Major industrial groups, apart from a few individuals, regarded the Fascist and Nazi movements with initial suspicion. Politicians like Giolitti, Salandra, Orlando and Nitti were much better known in industrial circles; in Germany the same could be said of Brüning (with reservations) and Papen. But Mussolini with his socialist past, and Hitler, an ill-educated Austrian from nowhere, were distinctly outsiders. Moreover, their movements were filled with equally marginal types. To complicate matters further, the Fascist and Nazi programmes contained many fuzzy ideas about the economy.

Nevertheless, industrial assistance to the Fascists and Nazis came in many forms. First, industrial pressure helped create the more general climate of anti-parliamentarianism and anti-socialism that bred authoritarian solutions. Second, some industrialists offered direct, limited financial assistance to both Fascists and Nazis. Mussolini's *Il Popolo d'Italia* had received money from industrialists like the Perrone brothers, who controlled the Ansaldo shipping and steel combine, and industrialist politician Dante Ferraris. Further industrial support came during the 1921 elections; subsequently, the Fascist deputies worked with industrial representatives in the Parliamentary Economic Alliance, a new pro-business grouping formed in 1922. Hitler assiduously courted the industrialists through intermediaries like Hjalmar Schacht and Wilhelm Funk and friendly industrialists like Emil Kirdorf and Fritz Thyssen. Hitler himself tried to reassure businessmen in a speech to the Industrial Club of Dusseldorf on 26 January 1932. While the overall significance of these contacts is in some dispute (Henry A. Turner and Paul Hayes point out that during the 1932 presidential election Krupp and Carl Duisberg of I.G. Farben came out for Hindenburg over Hitler, and Paul Reusch failed to work out a deal to support Hitler in March 1932), the Nazis had been legitimized in the eyes of the conservative and nationalist industrial establishment.[10]

At the moment of crisis of both the Italian and German parliamentary regimes, industrial groups pressed for a solution that at least included the Fascists and Nazis. No evidence exists, however, that they demanded either Mussolini or Hitler as heads of government. Italian industrialists would have preferred to find a way out of the crisis without necessarily leaving the constitutional order. Until the end, their candidate remained the aged Giolitti in some combination with Mussolini's Fascists. In Germany, the business interests would have liked the bourgeois parties to consolidate their position in the September 1930 elections and might have preferred other Nazis to Hitler. However, Italian and German business interests sought two contradictory things. They wanted to use the breakdown of the liberal party system in order to exclude the Socialist party and unions from any influence over political and economic policy, while at the same time finding a way back into modified parliamentary legality. Once the issue was framed in these terms, the response pointed directly to Mussolini and to Hitler.

The logic behind the inclusion of the PNF and NSDAP in the government was remarkably similar in both cases. Both provided a solution to problems of social order in the country and to a difficult parliamentary situation. All elements of the existing political class wanted them in, although some hoped to split the more 'reasonable' wing off from the uncontrollables. Just as Giolitti, Salandra, Orlando, Nitti (who also negotiated with D'Annunzio) and Facta engaged in *pourparlers* with various representatives of Mussolini, Schleicher negotiated with Gregor Strasser and Papen and Hugenberg dealt with Göring and Hitler on possible coalitions. The obvious desire of the existing political elites to have the Fascists and Nazis participate gave a kind of veto power to Mussolini and to Hitler. Mussolini and Göring, if not Hitler, sensed that their conservative partners were both desperate to exclude other rivals and eager to bring the Fascists and Nazis in and that they could insist on the top spot. Although both leaders got to the final point by mobilizing mass movements, the crisis that brought them to power was played out within an extremely small circle. In Italy, the king, his military advisers and Salandra made the crucial decisions; Hindenburg, State Secretary Otto Meissner, Papen and Hugenberg played similar roles in Germany. Whatever the Fascists and Nazis thought of themselves, the conservatives believed that they could stabilize the political system and the existing social order. Tim Mason's conclusion on the Nazi accession to power might well be applied to Fascist Italy as well:

> The most important preconditions for the rapid shift in the character of domination were, on the one hand, the development of the powerful National Socialist mass organizations in the years before 1933, which destroyed or 'co-ordinated' all oppositional groupings and, on the other hand, the self preservation and self-assertion within their own special spheres of interest and competence, of certain powerful organizations of the ruling classes (trade associations, cartels, the civil service, and the armed forces) and their active cooperation with the new dictatorship. These two preconditions were closely linked with each other; they were interdependent basic features of the economic and political crisis.[11]

4 The exercise of power

On 29 October 1922 Benito Mussolini at 39 years of age became the youngest prime minister in the brief history of united Italy. Just over ten years later on 30 January 1933, Hitler at age 44 also assumed office. Because they came to power by means of coalitions with the conservative political class, the basic political situation for both leaders was similar. However, the Nazi consolidation of power was compressed into a much shorter period of time. Two things account for this. First, as Tim Mason noted, the National Socialists had developed much further as a mass movement and therefore Hitler held a stronger position *vis-à-vis* his conservative allies. In 1922 Mussolini's party, though it was a substantial fighting force in the North and Centre, controlled but a small faction in parliament; the PNF had not penetrated in much of the South, and the conservative institutional structure was extremely strong. The Italian Statuto dating from 1848 was still in force and no case had been made for its total abandonment in order to return to strong government. Hitler had both the Italian and the Bolshevik models to draw upon in setting up a single party state, whereas Mussolini had been moving in uncharted waters with allies who were not at all convinced that the parliamentary system needed to be destroyed. In Germany, not only were the conservatives politically weaker, but they were less committed to the survival of the recently created Weimar constitution. Second, Germany still had a large and potentially powerful left-wing organizational structure. While the German Social Democrats had been marginalized in parliament, both the Socialists and the rapidly growing Communists still had their organizations largely in place. By the time the Italian Fascists had taken power, the left had been decimated in rural Italy and the urban labour organizations had lost much of their support.

On assuming power neither Mussolini nor Hitler was head of state, although the Führer would soon gain this office. In Italy the king remained the symbol of state authority throughout the life of the regime; in Germany the aged President Paul von Hindenburg lingered until July 1934. Significantly, the military command in both countries owed primary loyalty to the head of state.

In Italy, Mussolini took over the Presidency of the Council and the Ministries of the Interior and Foreign Affairs. Three other positions went to Fascists, including the Finance Ministry to Alberto De Stefani, a free market economist. The rest of the cabinet was made up of one Nationalist (Luigi Federzoni at the Ministry for Colonies), three Democrats, two members of the Catholic Popular Party, two military officers, and the philosopher Giovanni Gentile as Minister of Public Instruction. Reflecting the ideological ambiguities of fascism in 1922, Mussolini attempted to bring in Gino Baldesi, a reformist leader of the Socialist trade union confederation, but the attempt was blocked by Mussolini's conservative coalition partners and by Baldesi's own Unitary Socialist Party.

Hitler's coalition seemed on paper to give less power to the Nazis in 1933 than Mussolini had obtained in 1922. Hitler took the Chancellorship, but he was joined by only two other National Socialists: Göring as Reich Commissioner for both Air Transport and the Prussian Interior Ministry (a key post that controlled the largest police force in Germany), and Frick as Reich Interior Minister. The other positions went to conservatives: Constantin von Neurath at Foreign Affairs, Gürtner at Justice and Schwerin von Krosigk at Finance. The Nationalist Hugenberg became economic tsar with control of both the Agriculture and Economics Ministries and Papen was made Vice-Chancellor and Göring's nominal superior as Reich Commissioner for Prussia. The army remained where it had been, under the watchful if somewhat senile President von Hindenburg who dictated the choice of the War Minister.

Further parallels may be found in the conflicting pressures to which the new governments were subjected from the populist lower middle-class supporters who felt their moment had come to reap the rewards of battle. The Fascist and National Socialist leaders derived their autonomy *vis-à-vis* their conservative allies precisely from their ability to control and manoeuvre this mass base, yet the spoils of victory could not be had at the expense of alienating the broad spectrum of middle-class public opinion.

Both new governments were expected to resolve the parliamentary stalemate and to stabilize their political control. For Mussolini this task was both urgent and complicated; for Hitler with over one-third of the Reichstag at his command, the establishment of a firm majority was merely the prerequisite for executive government that could dispense entirely with parliamentary control.

As they dealt with political realities, managing conservative allies, unrest within their movements and consolidation of a parliamentary base – Mussolini and Hitler shared one asset. The economic crisis in both countries had bottomed out *before* the Fascists and National Socialists came to power. In 1922 Mussolini was going to profit from a strong recovery after the postwar recession; Hitler benefitted from policies put into place by his predecessors, Brüning and Papen.[1]

The fundamental problem for both Mussolini and Hitler upon taking power was to ensure that they would hold it permanently. Unlike the Bolsheviks who made their revolution against the existing social and economic order, the Fascists and National Socialists were forced to act with more circumspection. Ten years of experimentation by Mussolini in the techniques of authoritarian rule gave Hitler important advantages. In 1922, the Duce simply did not have a clear idea what outcome was possible. Speaking before parliament he stressed his determination to hold on to power, but the form of Fascist rule could not be known. Until the spring of 1924 Mussolini held out hopes for an alliance with part of the reformist labour unions. No consensus existed within the PNF. Some Fascists wanted total power and the suppression of parliament, while others envisaged no more than a reinvigorated executive within a reformed parliamentary system. A grant of decree-law power to the government by the legislature in November 1922 allowed the government to carry out economic and administrative reforms and to embark on a conservative restructuring of the educational system. But all of these initial moves could be easily assimilated within a conservative reworking of the constitution. What could not be considered as normalization was the continued brutal action of the Fascist squads against the socialist, communist and left-wing Catholic opposition throughout 1923.

Two other initiatives indicated that the Fascists had no intention of being bound by legality. The creation of the Fascist Grand Council on 15 December 1922 and of the Fascist Voluntary National Militia were efforts by Mussolini to gain more control over the movement that brought him to power. Inevitably, the Grand Council acted as a parallel Council of Ministers from which the non-fascist parties were excluded, and the militia represented the *de facto* legalization of the violence of the Fascist squads by transforming a party army into one acting under state protection and at the disposition of the Prime Minister. The very existence of these two institutions presaged a single party state.

In a move that revealed the ambiguity of 'fascist' movements with regard to the established political and constitutional order, Mussolini, as Hitler would do later, called new elections. The decision to go to the polls was part of the basic compromise with the older conservative parties. In July 1923, Mussolini's government proposed and parliament accepted the Acerbo law that gave two thirds of the seats in the lower house of parliament to the electoral list that won a plurality of votes.[2] In order to win approval of the new law Mussolini persuaded the Catholic Church to put pressure on the Popular party to accept the law. He then included many of the pre-fascist liberals in his national electoral list and won the endorsement of several former liberal prime ministers, but not Giolitti or Nitti.

The campaign of 1924 drove a wedge between Mussolini and the democratic opposition. Despite vote-stealing and intimidation, the Fascist National List failed to carry either Milan or Turin, but the Fascists swept much of the rest of the country, especially rural areas where counter-revolutionary terror had been effective in shattering the Socialist movement. Then, on 30 May 1924, the reformist Socialist Giacomo Matteotti courageously denounced the government's tactics in a scathing speech to the new parliament. On 10 June Matteotti was kidnapped and murdered. The judicial investigation led inexorably to the resignation of two close associates of Mussolini, Cesare Rossi and Giovanni Marinelli.

If the Duce's task had been complicated by the need for a new electoral law, the Nazis with the enthusiastic support of the conservative coalition partners were able to dissolve the Reichstag (parliament) on 31 January 1933 and set new elections for 5 March. Almost simultaneously new elections were also called for the

Prussian state government. A decree of 4 February, 'For the Protection of the German People' authorized the police to suppress newspapers and public meetings deemed to have directed attacks against the state.

On 27 February the Reichstag building was destroyed in a fire started by a Dutch Communist, Marinus van der Lubbe, acting independently of KPD or the Comintern. Although the Nazis initially believed in a Communist plot, they understood almost immediately that the fire could be used as a pretext for a general repression.[3] The basic law of the dictatorship, the emergency decree 'For the Defence of the Nation and State' of 28 February 1933, suspended the Weimar constitution and temporarily transferred all powers of the states (Länder) to the Reich government.

Despite a climate of extreme violence on the part of the National Socialists, the elections of 5 March 1933 gave the NSDAP 43.9 per cent and a bare 51.8 per cent majority with its Nationalist allies. Like the Fascists in 1924, the Nazis did poorly in the cities, with only 31.3 per cent of the vote in Berlin and 30.1 per cent in Cologne-Aachen.[4] Nor did the Nazis penetrate the Catholic areas to the same degree that they did Protestant regions.

The consequences of electoral victory were quite different for each regime. The crisis that resulted from the murder of Matteotti lasted from June to December 1924. Because it almost toppled Mussolini, it foreshadowed one of the fundamental weaknesses of Italian fascism *vis-à-vis* the more dynamic Nazi version. In order to placate the king and the conservative political establishment Mussolini relinquished control of the Interior Ministry and the police to a conservative monarchist, Luigi Federzoni, a former leader of the Italian Nationalist Association who had only joined the PNF in early 1923. Federzoni in turn replaced the Fascist police chief, Emilio De Bono with Francesco Crispo Moncada, a career bureaucrat. Thus a conservative held the Interior Ministry as the single party dictatorship emerged in 1925 and 1926. (Mussolini only regained control in late 1926.) Alfredo Rocco, another Nationalist who held the strategic Ministry of Justice until 1932, ensured that the repression would take place under the auspices of the traditional bureaucratic apparatus. Italy would have nothing comparable to the Nazi party SS organization, although its state security police, the OVRA, was comparable to the German Gestapo in function and effectiveness.

After the March 1933 elections the German government passed an Enabling Act, which vested in the government the right to decree constitutional changes. To win approval Hitler entered into direct negotiations with the Catholic bishops and the Vatican to circumvent opposition from the Catholic party. After promises to respect the Catholic schools and the rights of the Church in Bavaria, the Catholic Episcopal Conference called for cooperation with the new government. Here again, the Fascists and National Socialists, in consolidating their power, were forced to manoeuvre around powerful institutions rather than confront them directly.

With Hitler's government assured of a majority in a parliament largely deprived of its functions, political parties no longer served much purpose. The Communists had been banned after the Reichstag fire. In May 1933 the offices of the Free Trade Unions were occupied by Nazis and in June the SPD was outlawed. The same month the smaller bourgeois democratic parties (the State Party and the DVP), faced by Nazi threats and the collapse of their electorate, were dissolved along with the DNVP. The last to go was the Catholic Centre party, which self-liquidated in early July as part of the deal for a concordat between the Vatican and the Nazi regime. The completion of this process came on 14 July 1933 in the Law against the Establishment of Parties by which Germany officially became a one-party state. Although some conservatives remained in the government well into the 1930s, the architects of the alliance between the traditional right and Hitler, Papen and Hugenberg, lost their posts. The arrogant Hugenberg was dismissed on 26 June; Papen had handed power in Prussia over to Göring in April 1933 but held on as Vice-Chancellor until June 1934 when he barely escaped the Röhm purge with his life. No German conservatives ever had the power of Federzoni or Alfredo Rocco to make strategic and irreversible decisions about the nature of the dictatorship.

The Matteotti crisis rendered impossible a return to the uneasy balance between formal legality and Fascist criminality that had existed between October 1922 and June 1924. Most of the democratic opposition (except for the Communists and several key old-line politicians) withdrew from the Chamber of Deputies and called on the king to dismiss Mussolini. On the other side, hardline Fascists, led by Roberto Farinacci of Cremona, pressed for violent reprisals against the anti-fascists. However, the king and his advisers believed that the changes imposed on Mussolini at the beginning of the crisis would be sufficient. Mussolini ably reassured the Army, the Catholic Church and the industrialists of his intention to respect their traditional spheres of influence. Moreover, they believed that only he could hold in check the Fascist extremists who pressed to reopen the civil war. But the most important consideration in the eyes of the conservatives was the seeming inability of the anti-fascist opposition – an uneasy coalition of liberal democrats, socialists and democratic Catholics – to offer assurance that it could govern when politicians of the older generation had already tried and failed.

On 3 January 1925, Mussolini, confidence restored, challenged his opponents to remove him or stand aside. Interior Minister Federzoni activated a press decree that allowed seizure of opposition newspapers. Public meetings, even those held by the Fascist Party, were banned. In February 1925 the extremist Farinacci was appointed Secretary-General of the Fascist Party to counter-balance the influence of Federzoni and to keep the pent-up frustration of the provincial base of the party from exploding against the conservative establishment. Although the *ras* of Cremona was the spokesman of provincial radicalism, Mussolini judged Farinacci's authoritarian personality accurately. The new secretary of the PNF clearly wanted the party, not the state bureaucracy, to be the driving force of the emerging regime, but he used his power to centralize, discipline and drain the spontaneity from the party. Henceforth all offices were filled by appointment rather than election; commands replaced discussion. On 30 April 1926, just when Farinacci seemed to be building his own political apparatus, Mussolini replaced him.

By the time Federzoni was dismissed in November 1926 after a series of attempts on the Duce's life, the framework of the Fascist state was already in place. The key legislative and executive actions that established the Fascist authoritarian structure came in two waves. In November and December 1925, after an assassination attempt on Mussolini by Tito Zaniboni, a social democratic politician, parliamentary government was ended by the Law on the Powers of the Head of Government. The old *primus inter pares* presidency of the Council of Ministers was abolished in favour of a system that subordinated the cabinet to the newly created office of Head of Government, responsible only to the king. Zaniboni's party, the Unitary Socialist Party, was also outlawed. Laws passed against secret societies at this time allowed for a purge of the bureaucracy, although, as in Nazi Germany, such purges were quite limited in practice.[5]

In November 1926, after yet another attempt on Mussolini's life, the surviving political parties were abolished. December brought the Law for the Defence of the State that established the political police (OVRA) and a Special Tribunal to handle the newly defined political crimes. Throughout 1925 and 1926 elected local government had been replaced by appointed officials; most professional associations aligned themselves with the new reality by adding the term 'fascist' to their name. The opposition press disappeared: that of the parties was suppressed along with the sponsoring political organization; the independent press followed its industrial and financial owners in support of the regime.

5 The new order

The fascist form of rule involved three closely related factors: the role of the supreme leader; highly informal and unsystematic constitutional and institutional practice; and a constantly shifting party-state relationship. Both regimes were personal dictatorships in which the supreme leader was the ultimate arbiter. Mussolini was far more involved in the ordinary processes of governing, at least through the early 1930s, than was Hitler. In fact, at various times the Duce personally held several important Cabinet Ministries: the War, Navy and Air Force Ministries from 1925 to 1929 and again from 1933 to 1943, the Foreign Ministry from 1924 to 1929 and from July 1932 to June 1936, the Interior Ministry from October 1922 to June 1924 and from November 1926 to July 1943, the Ministry of Corporations from July 1926 to September 1929 and from July 1932 to June 1936. Because of this accumulation of offices an incredible amount of material passed through the Duce's secretariat, even to decisions on when the Rome traffic police might switch to summer uniforms. But supervision of ministerial bureaucracy was only part of the problem. Mussolini had contempt for and distrusted his subordinates. 'Unlike Hitler who allowed prominent Nazis to build political and economic power centres (Göring in the Four Year Plan and in his vast holding company, Fritz Todt in construction, Himmler in the police and the SS)', the Italian leader pushed aside anyone in the party who threatened to develop an independent political base.

Hitler, through natural indolence and personal style, tended to be more remote from the execution of policy. The Führer preferred to issue general directives and to delay decisions in the hope that lower-level officials would arrive at some sort of consensus. As a result, middle-level bureaucrats had considerable room for initiatives. But even Hitler could become highly agitated when a subject touched certain areas, as witnessed by a memo from Martin Bormann to Robert Ley:

> For your information the Führer wishes to see an end to the use of waiters in all restaurants. The job of waiter is, in the Führer's view, not the right sort of work for a man but rather appropriate work for women and girls.[1]

Yet despite differences in personal style, the systems created by Mussolini and Hitler were alike in basic form. Power in the fascist dictatorships never ran horizontally. All official relations were bilateral or vertically directed through the person of the Duce or the Führer, who retained the final word on all important matters. Despite the debates over Hitler's role as a weak or strong dictator or over how much policy was the result of a specific intention of the leader rather than the product of manoeuvering among powerful fiefdoms, little doubt exists that Hitler and Mussolini set the basic foreign policy goals of their regimes and inspired the social and economic policies necessary to implement them.[2] But, in the case of Nazi Germany, setting broad policy goals and leaving implementation to a number of competing power centres resulted in wasteful and chaotic government. In Fascist Italy the Duce's tendency to control everything in a superficial way led to a regime in which no one really took risks to change the status quo. It was a style that played into the hands of conservative established social and economic fiefdoms.

Rather than deal with one another in formal constitutional ways, significant interest groups tended to negotiate in an informal or extra-constitutional manner. Each competing interest group remained theoretically autonomous within its sphere. If informal negotiations did not resolve conflict, an appeal to the leader was a last resort. Ian Kershaw aptly described the situation in Nazi Germany:

> It was not in itself simply the undermining of 'rational' structures of government and the proliferation of chaotic, 'polycratic' agencies that mattered. It was that the process accompanied and promoted a gradual realization of ideological aims

which were inexorably bound up in the 'mission' of the 'charismatic' Leader, as the idea of Nazism, located in the person of the Führer, became translated between 1938 and 1942 from utopian 'vision' into practical reality. There was, in other words, a symbiotic relationship between the structural disorder of the Nazi state and the radicalization of policy.[3]

Government bodies, such as parliament or the Council of Ministers, within which issues could be debated and compromises reached, ceased to play a significant role. Parliament lost much of its function in both regimes with the onset of one party government, although it continued to meet. The cabinet also slipped into irrelevance. The German cabinet met 72 times in 1933, 19 in 1934. In 1937 it had only 7 meetings. Hitler held no cabinet meetings after 1938. Nothing replaced it and Hitler's absence from Berlin after the late 1930s made any regular government difficult in any case. Mussolini, who controlled several key ministries, could hold virtual cabinet meetings in his head. However, before the onset of personal rule, the Duce chaired seventy cabinet meetings in 1933 but only four in 1936. At the time of the outbreak of the Second World War in September 1939, the cabinet met without ever discussing the international situation. Even though the Fascist Grand Council convened only when Mussolini wished and had its membership dictated by the Duce, it too slipped into irrelevance and met infrequently as the 1930s went on.

Thus, instead of a coherent and unified system, both regimes turned over administrative and even quasi-legislative powers to new agencies or to economic and political interest groups on an *ad hoc* basis. Powerful state and private interest groups manoeuvred to establish their spheres of influence in the absence of formal legislative or cabinet action. In the early days of the Third Reich industrial leaders won a substantial victory with the Law on the Reordering of National Labour, which shifted power within factories from unions to management. Robert Ley's Labour Front was specifically excluded from interfering in negotiations over wages and working conditions. Ley retaliated by getting a Führer decree directly from Hitler in October 1934 that gave the Labour Front some attributes of a union by allowing it to intervene in factory management. Because a Hitler decree could never be rescinded and the earlier law was on the books, a permanent conflict was built into the Nazi system.[4] During the Second World War Carlo Scorza, the secretary of the PNF, complained to Mussolini about a long-standing problem in the system:

> The various ministries appear today as a tangle of ill-defined and more often conflicting functions which complicate the conduct of the simplest business. I add that – frequently – such interferences are eliminated and the business concluded on the basis of a common and by now widespread private negotiation, that is to say, exchange of personal favours and circulation of money.[5]

Ian Kershaw caught the essential anarchy in the fascist system of rule:

> The proliferation of 'special authorities' and plenipotentiaries for special tasks, delegated by the Führer and responsible directly to him, reflected the predatory character and improvised techniques immanent in Nazi domination. Lack of coherent planning related to attainable middle-range goals, absence of any forum for collective decision-making, the arbitrary exercise of power embedded in the 'leadership principle' at all levels; the Darwinian principle of unchecked struggle and competition until the winner emerged; and the simplistic belief in the 'triumph of the will', whatever the complexities to be overcome; all these reinforced each other and interacted to guarantee a jungle of competing and overlapping agencies of rule.[6]

This fragmentation of the state was the result of the personal proclivities of the Duce and the Führer, an inability to dispense with established social and economic elites, and a strategic decision to concentrate on foreign and military policy. Foreign policy, however, played a much more limited role in Fascist Italy until 1934. During the 1920s and early 1930s the Duce acted under the constraints of an unfavourable international balance of power and of the domestic compromises that he made as he re-established his authority after the Matteotti crisis. Ironically, his regime was far more stable when he operated under thse limitations. By the early 1930s he had created an authoritarian regime whose stability had been purchased in part at the expense of fascism's totalitarian aspirations. As we shall see, Mussolini began to undermine this system after 1935.

The fascist style of government left major institutions in constant flux, making it difficult to appeal to constitutional procedure for vindication. Both regimes embarked on the creation of their new state on an *ad hoc* basis, as befitting regimes that glorified instinct and will over reason and legal norms. To have drafted an entirely new constitution in either Italy or Germany involved many economic, social and political issues better left undefined until the new order was fully consolidated. Thus neither regime formally replaced the old constitution with a new one. For example, the Nazis never bothered to abolish the old states of Germany, even after they had been drained of real power in March and April 1933. The January 1934 Law for the Reconstruction of the Reich left the Länder as sinecures for powerful Nazi provincial leaders. Italy's King Victor Emmanuel contended just before the Second World War that the entire Fascist dictatorship could be reversed by a single decree – something that he finally did in July 1943. But Fascist Italy was beset by deeper and more confusing political loyalties than was Nazi Germany. Alongside the traditional court hierarchy and etiquette determined by the king, a separate system of Fascist hierarchies and honours developed, just as religious authorities and local Fascist leaders competed with their rival calendars of 'holy days'. In contrast, after the death of Marshal von Hindenburg in July 1934, a law passed on 1 August vested all presidential powers in the newly created office of the Führer. In the process, Hitler became both Head of State and Government. Mussolini, though freed from any parliamentary control as Head of Government, was formally more akin to a Prime Minister.

Understandably, in light of the delicate issue involved, no line of succession for the office of Duce or Führer was determined in Italy or Germany. Mussolini never wanted the Fascist Grand Council to develop any independent initiative. Thus, in 1928, when it was given constitutional authority to draft a list of successors to the Duce, Mussolini saw to it that it would never compile such a list. Potential rivals, like Italo Balbo, the charismatic head of the air force, were sent off to various gilded exiles. Hitler's choice of the relatively weak Rudolf Hess as Vice-Führer merely ensured that the sucession issue would remain open. On the eve of the war, in typically confusing fashion Hitler named both Hess and Göring as his potential successors and, when the more than slightly daft Hess departed on his mission to Britain, Göring was left in sole possession of the honour. Though Hitler remained loyal to the core of Nazi leaders and allowed them vast personal fiefdoms, he was just as determined as Mussolini that no challenger should emerge from the NSDAP. He did not even experiment with collegial organs like the Fascist Grand Council.

6　The institutionalization
of the party

Much uncertainty existed as to how the Fascist and Nazi parties might be assimilated into the state. The simplest way would have been to replace the existing administrative class with militants from the PNF and NSDAP. This was not desirable for at least three related reasons. First, it conflicted with the vision that the more radical and populist elements in the two parties had for themselves. To be forced to submit to regular procedures and routines was at odds with the rebellious 'fascist' mentality. Second, both Hitler and Mussolini mistrusted the professional civil service because the bureaucracies were full of opportunists and fellow travellers who joined the movements after they had already succeeded. Finally, the PNF and NSDAP simply lacked the technical abilities to run the state. At best, the party could act as guardian of the so-called 'revolution', but to accomplish even this task it had to be reorganized and centralized. For various reasons, however, neither Mussolini nor Hitler wanted to entrust the party with this much initiative.

As they worked to insert the Fascist and Nazi parties into the governmental apparatus, the leaders confronted a serious problem. Their movements had been combat forces, more suited for mass mobilization and street fighting than for governing. The difficulty in Italy, as it would be in Germany, was to find a role for the party militants that did not interfere with the working of the government. Above all, the uncontrollable and violent factions in the party base had to be domesticated. During the weeks after the March on Rome, Fascist squads went on a rampage of pillage and murder in centres including Turin and Florence before a shocked foreign press. Similar occurences happened in early 1933 in Germany.

Local party officials and the SA terrorized working-class quarters and created concentration camps where the torture of left-wing militants was routine. Public opinion accepted some of this violence against the left but drew the line when the attacks spread to department stores and an ill-conceived boycott of Jewish-owned businesses on 1 April. Local governments that had hired SA thugs soon tired of the violence and extortion. Both Mussolini and Hitler drew back. The Italian leader sought to gain some measure of control in January 1923 with the formation of the Fascist National Voluntary Militia (MVSN). Hitler found himself deluged by protests. Convinced that the populist attacks on such a large scale provoked an adverse reaction in domestic and foreign public opinion, the Führer reined in the party base in mid-1933, built up the rival SS, and eventually purged the SA leadership at the end of June 1934.

On taking power, the Nazis and the Fascists had no alternative but to defer to bureaucrats, conservative allies or recent converts to the movement. A Fascist law of December 1925 and the Nazi Law for the Restoration of the Professional Civil Service of 7 April 1933, both designed to purge the bureaucracy, had relatively limited impact, since most civil servants were politically conservative and nationalist. In Italy after 1925 and in Germany after mid-1933 there was a massive influx of civil servants into the party ranks. The old bureaucratic hierarchies remained in place in the established Ministries of Foreign Affairs, Finance, Interior and Justice where a strong professional component existed. For obvious reasons, newly created ministries, like Goebbels' Propaganda Ministry or the Fascist Ministry of Corporations, could most easily be politicized outside of civil service rules.

The danger that the old guard would be swamped by opportunistic new adherents was very real. A debate took place in both parties over whether the movement would remain an elite force in society or a mass party that would virtually reflect the entire population. The Fascists and Nazis were ambivalent. In Italy, Fascists like Giuseppe Bottai and Massimo Rocca argued for an elite party that would form the core of a new political class. Similar debates took place in Nazi Germany where Hess and Bormann argued for an elite party that would control society in contrast to those like Robert Ley, the head of the Labor Front, who wanted a mass movement. Initially, mass prevailed. The NSDAP grew from 130,000 in September 1930 to 850,000 in January 1933 to 2.5 million at the beginning of 1935, when limits were placed on new memberships. Controls lasted for two years during which access was mainly through passage from Hitler Youth to the party. Removal of limitations in 1937 led to an explosion of members to 5.3 million in 1939 and 7.1 million in 1942.

The Fascist Party increased more slowly from 500,000 in October 1922 to almost a million in 1926. Much of the debate within the PNF in 1923 and 1924 revolved around its potential role as a political elite and what the influx of new members might mean for this mission. After 1926 the Grand Council decreed that further membership would be limited to those who graduated from the youth organizations. Party Secretary Augusto Turati selectively sought to expand the party's membership in middle-class elite groups. However, limits were lifted in 1932 in an effort to bring in all civil servants. Then, during the 1930s all selectivity was lost. By 1939 the party was on paper a formidable organization of 2.6 million members and would grow even larger with the admission of military personnel. At that point, the PNF was a huge operation but it could no longer serve as an incubator of a new political elite. A measure of its insignificance came in July 1943 when the party received news of Mussolini's removal by a Grand Council vote without lifting a finger in defence of the Duce.

Still, no organization of the size of both the NSDAP and the PNF could be entirely without an important role. Both parties became bureaucracies that extended down to the neighbourhood level. They had important roles in dispensing charity, overseeing price regulations and campaigns against hoarding, and enforcing racial policy, the new linguistic regulations and leading patriotic drives for the war effort. Thus, the party became a major means by which both regimes sought to create a new kind of Italian or German citizen.

The integration of Fascist and Nazi party members into the state's administrative apparatus took place most extensively on the local level. In Italy, the Fascist squads had already beaten the left and had inherited many of its positions. Town councils in the hands of opponents were dissolved by friendly prefects acting on orders from the government. Where a direct takeover was difficult or undesirable, the PNF and the NSDAP developed new party organs that assumed quasi-governmental roles. The Grand Council authorized the creation of political commissars, *alti commissari*, for regions and provinces, as another way of rewarding the most powerful local *ras*. Though potentially quite powerful, the commissars interfered with the prefects, caused administrative chaos and raised objections from conservative allies of the government. The experiment was rapidly abandoned and eventually Mussolini issued a circular in January 1927 that reaffirmed the authority of the prefects over party officials in the various provinces.

From the late 1920s on, party representatives in Italy sat on local intersyndical committees that often intervened in local economic disputes and supervised prices and wages. The PNF also ran the leisure-time organization, the Opera Nazionale Dopolavoro (OND), which had 4 million members, and in 1937 all youth organizations were transferred from the Ministry of National Education to the party-controlled Gioventù Italiana del Littorio (GIL). Finally, in 1939 the PNF and the Fascist unions gained the right to have their representatives within individual plants supervise the application of labour contracts. From 1925 to 1939 no union presence was allowed in the factories. Contracts were worked out nationally or by province, but the union role stopped at the factory gate.

In Germany on the local and provincial level, a massive takeover of formerly political and elective offices by the party faithful also occurred. It started at the top with Hitler as both party Führer and Chancellor. The various Gauleiters were made Reichsstatthalter (Reich governors) of the Länder by a law of 7 April 1933. (In Prussian territory the Gauleiters were made Oberpraesidenten of the various Prussian provinces.) District party leaders (Kreileiter) became Oberburgermeister or Landräte.

By the late 1930s, the Nazi party, a hierarchy that numbered 700,000 people, penetrated all levels of society from regions and districts down to party cells and block groups. At the base of the party were hundreds of thousands full- and part-time workers whose role was to watch over and report on the conduct of their neighbours and to work on the process of re-education – enforcing the racial campaigns, economic measures and new linguistic policies. On the next level, heads of party cells, the NSDAP had 90,000 organizers. The heads of local Nazi party branches, roughly 20,000 to 30,000, were all full-time and served as conduits for those who sought employment in local government. There were 827 Kreis or district leaders who arranged major party events. At the top were the 33 Gauleiters.[1] Of course, this party hierarchy did not include the auxiliary women's, leisure-time and youth organizations, nor did it include the SA and SS membership. The Fascist and Nazi parties served as rich sources of patronage. Jane Caplan notes that the Nazi party and its various specialized organs (labour, women's and youth organizations, leisure-time organizations and welfare activities) employed over 1 million people. The Fascist Party bureaucracy grew in a similar manner.[2]

Both Hitler and Mussolini were determined to control their parties and bend them to a supreme will. This process was not as simple as it seemed. Party aspirations and grievances that operated independently of the ambitions of the Duce or Führer had to be reined in. Indicative of Mussolini's reluctance to put too much political power into the hands of the party was the fact that the Duce himself held the Interior Ministry post from 1926 to 1943. Under these circumstances, no Fascist Party challenge to the police powers of the Interior Ministry was possible. Nor would the Duce appoint a truly able National Secretary of the Fascist Party after 1930. A number of competent leaders, for example Giuseppe Bottai and Dino Grandi, wanted the job, but Mussolini preferred politically weaker and less dynamic men. One exception, the appointment of Roberto Farinacci in 1925, was made in order to discipline the unruly squads. Within a year Farinacci was replaced by the competent but no less ambitious August Turati, the leader of Brecian fascism. Turati fell out of favour when he tried to combine the position of Party Secretary with that of Under-Secretary at the Interior Ministry. With Mussolini as Duce and Interior Minister, Turati would have automatically become the Deputy Duce. Rather than allow this, Mussolini replaced Turati with the colourless Giovanni Giuriati, an ex-member of the Italian Nationalist Association with no real standing in the party, and then with the grotesque Achille Starace. In the process, the PNF was diminished as a power centre and as an incubator of a new political class, even as it enlarged its role as a mass movement with a mission of re-educating Italians.

A major effort to rationalize the NSDAP's structure came before January 1933 when Gregor Strasser, then head of the Political Organization, developed a coherent strategy to unify the party. When Strasser's challenge to Hitler's leadership fizzled in December 1932, Robert Ley replaced him, but Ley had none of the skills or prestige of Strasser and, in a typical maneouvre, Hitler balanced the Political Organization with the new office of Deputy Führer.

Essentially, Hitler preferred to control the party through the Führer principle and his personal ties to old fighters, augmented by Hess's office of Deputy Führer and that of the Party Treasurer, Franz Xavier Schwarz, who kept local party organizations on a tight financial leash. Hess's operation was one of potential political importance because he was given a central government role almost immediately. The Deputy Führer had the right from July 1934 to participate in the drafting of all laws and to pass on major civil service appointments in all ministries. Hess's powers clearly overlapped with those of Interior Minister Wilhelm Frick, whose plans to centralize administrative authority in his ministry were stymied. In short, Hitler thwarted the projects of the Reich Interior Ministry to take over the Nazi revolution, but he left the party in disarray. Initially, the Fascist Party Secretary did not get these extensive governmental powers. However, the party statute of 1929 considerably increased the importance of the PNF Secretary. The appointment was made by royal decree on the recommendation of the Head of Government. In addition, he was to be the Secretary of the Grand Council and could participate in the Council of Ministers, the Supreme Defence Council, the National Council of Corporations and the Central Corporative Committee.

Out of necessity, but also partly out of distrust of the traditional bureaucracy, both regimes set up a number of specialized state and parastate agencies under the control of leading party members. Older governmental organs were allowed to drift aimlessly or were incorporated into new agencies or super-ministries that reported to the supreme leader. These newer bureaucracies, more susceptible to party influence than the traditional ministries, were of four types: party-political, welfare, economic and security. Some of these, especially those dealing with social welfare and economics appeared in all industrialized countries during the 1930s.

What made the 'Fascist' system unique were the vertical authoritarian context within which institutions developed and the almost Hobbesian struggle between leaders who were forced to compete for the favour of the supreme leader without any fixed rules to regulate the competition. For instance, by 1942 eleven new Reich-level agencies had been created over and alongside existing ministries. The Four Year Plan alone had seventeen subordinate agencies. In Italy six ministries competed with a number of special-ized agencies and directorates for control of the economy. Only firm direction from Mussolini or Hitler could hold such a chaotic structure together, but by the outbreak of the Second World War they were far too distracted to provide it.

In both Italy and Germany the political administrative apparatus of the party paralleled that of the state on two levels: geograph-ical and functional. In both countries, provincial chiefs, the *ras* and the Gauleiter, continued to enjoy significant power in their own fiefdoms. In Germany, key Gauleiters combined their party offices with appointments as Reich governors. The durability of the old-line provincial leaders can be attributed to a shared personality trait in both Mussolini and (even more) in Hitler. Both men tended to avoid open conflicts with long-time associates who did not challenge them directly. For example, even after Farinacci had been removed as Party Secretary, he remained unchallenged in Cremona, although Mussolini detested him. Similarly, Italo Balbo dominated Ferrara's politics from his gilded exile as Governor of Libya. However, where a challenge was perceived, all power was removed. Such was the fate of Leandro Arpinati, Mussolini's Under-Secretary at the Interior, who lost a battle with Starace in 1933 and 1934 and to Augusto Turati whose power in Brescia was diminished after his removal as party secretary.

Powerful Gauleiters, like Erich Koch in East Prussia, Helmuth Brückner in Silesia, Wilhelm Kube in Brandenburg, and Adolf Wagner in Munich were able to defy government and party offi-cials because of their special relationship with Hitler. In the final analysis, the ultimate key to success in the Nazi regime was access to the Führer. The relatively obscure Martin Bormann, who replaced Hess as Hitler's private secretary, used this access to build up an extremely powerful position. To a lesser extent, on the governmental side, State Secretary Hans Lammers played a key role because he translated Hitler's rambles into legislative decrees.

7 The Fascist and Nazi economic systems

Industry

The Fascist and Nazi regimes worked from common principles but with strikingly different results as they developed their relationship with pre-existing elites in industry and agriculture. Both operated from a basic social Darwinist view of human relations. The aim was to expand industrial and agricultural production as far as possible without regard to weaker individuals and groups. In a system that had crippled the capacity of labour to defend its interests, this attitude ensured that management reaped greater benefits than the workers. Neither regime questioned private property and initiative, but, at the same time, the market system no longer regulated the economy. The entire industrial and agricultural capacity of the state was subordinated to the goals set by the political leadership.[1]

The Italian Fascist regime offered three major advantages to business interests. First, the power of the Socialist Party and of its General Confederation of Labour was broken despite efforts by the latter to find some sort of accommodation with the regime. Labour as an independent interest group was eliminated. Some in industry feared that the Fascist Labour Confederation, headed by Edmondo Rossoni, might replace the socialist organizations. In fact, Rossoni sought to do just that. In the Palazzo Vidoni agreement of 2 October 1925, the industrialists were forced to grant to the Fascist unions exclusive bargaining rights. Alfredo Rocco's labour legislation of 3 April 1926 officially recognized one labour and management association as bargaining agents in their respective spheres. However, the danger of a single dominant Fascist labour union was removed in 1928 when Rossoni lost the power struggle and the large Fascist union movement was broken into six weaker and smaller federations.

As in Fascist Italy, German industrial managers feared the formation of a powerful Nazi labour organization. An immediate gain from the Nazi victory was the destruction of independent trade unions, notably the large Socialist ADGB, which was taken over on 2 May 1933. The leader of the unions, Theodor Leipart, tried to separate his organization from the Socialist party and gain the protection of President Hindenburg, but to no avail. The SA and the Nazi Factory Cell Organization (NSBO) occupied all the offices of the Socialist unions and then merged the remaining independent and Catholic unions into the Labour Front, which had been formed on 6 May under Robert Ley, the head of the party political organization and future Labour Minister. The strength of the more radical NSBO, which reached a membership of 1 million by autumn 1933, was troubling to employers. Faced with a potential problem, Hitler, as did Mussolini before him, began the process of curbing Nazi labour organizations. The Law on Trustees of Labour of 19 May 1933 eliminated the bargaining functions of both the NSBO and the DAF by transferring power to set wages to officials under the Ministry of Labour, but this ministry was no longer the socialist stronghold it had been under Weimar. The new labour trustees were now associated with the employers and with an anti-labour regime. Although Ley was ordered to keep his Labour Front out of factory management, he managed to win a partial reversal of this decision with a personal appeal to Hitler, but the DAF never functioned as a normal trade union. In November 1933 the more radical elements were ousted from the NSBO and it was integrated into the DAF.[2] Despite its inability to negotiate with employers, the DAF grew into an organization of 45,000 permanent staff and a budget three times greater than that of the Nazi party. The Fascist and Nazi labour organizations themselves became hiring halls for legions of aspiring bureaucrats.

The second major gain for business under fascism was the destruction of union power within the factory itself. The Vidoni agreement of October 1925 ratified the dismantling of the factory councils through which the unions operated to supervise fulfillment of national contracts in individual factories. From 1925 until the late 1930s when shop representatives of the Fascist unions were again introduced into the workplace, employers were given unchallenged control within the firm. Unlike the Nazi Labour Front, Fascist unions kept nominal collective bargaining functions. National and provincial contracts were negotiated by the single syndical federations for labour and management. Disputes were passed on to labour courts, which could impose binding arbitration. Two additional factors negated labour's power. First, government-imposed wage and price reductions after 1927 set strict limits on the ability of Fascist unions to negotiate in favour of their members. Second, Fascist Italy in stark contrast to Nazi Germany, failed to bring down its rate of unemployment. The Fascist regime remained mired in the depression until preparations for war in Ethiopia provided a boost to the economy; in contrast, Nazi Germany moved into a recovery phase almost immediately on Hitler's assumption of power. The official rate of Italian unemployment stood at 181,493 in December 1926. With the onset of deflation in 1927 it rose to 414,283. By February 1933, well over 1 million were unemployed and the rates remained between 11 and 15 per cent into 1935 when mobilization for war began to kick in. But official statistics masked very high rates of under- and part-time employment. In contrast, from a high of 5.6 million out of work in 1932, Germany's unemployment rate fell to a point where it was statistically irrelevant after 1936. Labour shortages led to increased real wages from 1936 to 1939 despite the regime's efforts to hold down the process, although some of these gains were offset by food and housing shortages.

Finally, big business immediately gained a number of favourable legislative and administrative rulings. The Mussolini government ended the investigation into excess war profits and abandoned the effort to force registration of ownership of all stocks and bonds. Heavy industry benefitted from the revaluation of the lira in 1926. Deflation weeded out the weaker and smaller firms and consolidated major sectors of the economy in production and marketing cartels. A 1932 law further entrenched oligopolistic positions by authorizing the government to impose obligatory cartels. Employers were no longer subject to fines and penal sanctions for defaulting on payment of contributions to the unemployment insurance fund. New measures of social control over workers were also promulgated. In 1933 the workbook, a record to be carried by each worker, was instituted in order to claim social insurance benefits.

German industrialists had good reason to be content with the deflationary wage and tax policies already in place under Brüning and Papen. Thus from a strictly economic point of view the Nazis initially marked a step backward in two ways. Unlike the fascists, who abandoned the radical programme of 1919 and posed little threat to industrial and financial interests, the Nazi movement continued to be filled with fuzzy-minded populist types like Gottfried Feder and Otto Wagener who fueled the anti-capitalist aspirations of the NSDAP's Mittelstand base. On taking power, racial Nazis launched a campaign against department stores, which were hit with special tax legislation and by consumer boycotts. Artisan and small business groups sought to ban certain services from large chain stores and cooperatives. Even the concept of the industrial corporation was challenged by Nazi populists who dreamed of a return to the old guild system of patriarchal management.

Almost immediately, the NSDAP leaders were forced to choose between economic chaos implied in the anti-capitalist programme of the Mittelstand organizations and collaboration with the industrial sector in the pursuit of economic recovery and military rearmament. There was really no choice at all. Radical economic experimentation was never as central to Nazi ideology as were anti-Semitism, racial purity and eastward expansion. In July 1933 the brakes were slammed on hard. Kurt Schmitt, an executive of the Allianz Insurance Company, replaced Hugenberg as Minister of Economics and moved quickly to smooth relations with industry. In gratitude for the changed atmosphere, industrialists under the leadership of Krupp created the Adolf Hitler Donation, an assessment from industrial firms for the Nazi party. But things only got better. The battle against the department stores was called off. In August 1933 the populist Fighting Organization of the Industrial Middle Classes, which had organized the anti-department store campaign, was merged into the NS Hago, a party organization for trade and small business.

Although the offensive of Nazi radicalism was defeated, small businesses and artisans did win a few concessions. Existing department stores survived but no new ones were allowed. A Law for the Provisional Construction of the German Craft Trades of 29 November 1933 restored the old guild system for many of the artisinal trades. Despite the rhetoric, the Nazi state pressed ahead with the process of rationalizing the small business sector. There were 1.5 million small businesses – far too many. In 1936, 28,000 artisan workshops were closed and between 1937 and 1938 another 63,000 were shut down. Many remaining craft shops shifted to war production. Uniform makers, small parts manufacturers and the like did extremely well in the new climate.[3]

With the elimination of trade union power, the only threat to industrial autonomy in Fascist Italy arose from the state bureaucracy itself through the newly established corporative system. Corporativism can be described as a system of institutional arrangements by which capital and labour are integrated into officially recognized, obligatory, hierarchical and functional units, known as corporations. These corporations then become self-governing organs for issues relating to the specific sector, as well as the basis for participation with other corporatively organized interests in policy decisions affecting the entire society through the corporative parliament. Individuals would no longer be represented by geographical units, as in most liberal democratic systems, but through their workplace. Class conflict would be replaced by class harmony within the corporative structures.

In 1926 the Ministry of Corporations was created as a first step in the formation of a full-blown corporative society. If taken seriously, the corporative system would have allowed worker participation in management decisions to re-enter through the back door, and would have given a substantial role to state planners to mediate between capital and labour. Despite the hopes of those who equated fascism and corporativism and believed that it might be a 'third way' between capitalism and communism, Mussolini had no intention of moving to a true coporative state. In 1928 the breakup of the Fascist union structure fatally undermined labour's position in the new system. Between 1929 and 1932 a serious attempt was made to enlarge the role of the Ministry of Corporations, but that was thwarted in 1932 with the dismissal of Giuseppe Bottai, the ambitious, technocratic Minister of Corporations. Industrialists successfully opposed any institutional arrangements that shared power with workers or with the state bureaucracy. The corporative legislation of 1934 created a highly visible but essentially weak system of twenty-two corporations, divided into three large sectors of industry, agriculture and services. They had nominal control over wages and working conditions within the sector, but, in reality, only management profited from the system that acted as a cover for cartelization.

The final indication that no serious attempt would be made to disturb industrial autonomy came with the creation of the Istituto per la Ricostruzione Industriale (IRI) in January 1933. The IRI was a response to the Great Depression and the collapse of the Italian banking system. In 1931 the government began to manage the major banks by means of the Istituto Mobiliare Italiano (IMI). The process was completed with the 1936 Banking Reform Act by which the Bank of Italy and most of the other major banks became public institutions. The banking system was separated from long-term industrial financing. Both the IMI and the Bank Reform of 1936 resembled similar measures taken in other industrial societies and have not been viewed as particularly fascist solutions; in fact, the banking and industrial structures established in the 1930s continued after 1946 under the Republic.

When the banking system collapsed under the impact of the Great Depression in 1931 and 1932, the government found itself in control of stock portfolios that gave it operational control of major industrial corporations. Indirectly, the Fascist government had nationalized a large part of Italian industry. The IRI, which still exists, was a holding company set up to manage this state-controlled industrial sector. The decision to keep it outside of the corporative experiment and to place it under the direction of industrialist Alberto Beneduce symbolized the conservative orientation of the bail-out of 1933. When the shift to a war economy took place a few years later, the IRI and its subsidiary companies for steel, shipping, engineering and construction were able to play a large role in the drive for autarky.

Nazi Germany did not even pay lip-service to corporative ideology. In June and July 1933 the new relationship with industry was solidified when the Reich Association of German Industry became the Reich Estate of German Industry. Private firms were encouraged to organize into producer cartels by the Law for the Organic Construction of the German Economy of 27 February 1934. As in Italy, these cartels were built into a system of rearmament and state procurement and further entrenched dominant positions in all key sectors of the economy. In 1934 Schmitt was replaced as Economics Minister when he attacked the concentration of power in the Industrial Estate. In July, Schacht was appointed Economics Minister while keeping his post as President of the Reichsbank. From 1934 to 1936, he became a virtual economic tsar. Thus the decision was made to move ahead with the main lines of the Nazi programme within the existing industrial system. Up to this point, no divergence of views existed among industry, the military and the government over the objective of rearmament with an emphasis on the recovery of the heavy industrial sector.

Until 1936, the Fascist and Nazi models were quite similar. Whatever remained of corporative planning in Italy and Germany became a front for the cartelization of the economy. In both regimes worker organizations were substantially weakened and the authority of management strengthened within the plant. The social control exercised over the working class gave both regimes wide powers to suppress private consumption and to shift resources to industrial mobilization for war. Rationalization of labour, piece-work rates and time management could be introduced in both regimes without objections from trades unions. The Fascist syndical organizations offered scant protection. The PNF took over propagandistic and leisure-time activities with its affiliated Opera Nazionale Dopolavoro. The Nazi DAF and the Kraft Durch Freude filled a similar function. Both organizations offered subsidized vacations, summer camps and films in an effort to establish a new worker-management relationship based on issues unrelated to classic trade union collective bargaining.

Agriculture

As with industry, the Fascists and the Nazis moved quickly to aid the agricultural sector. The outcome was similar, even if the rewards were somewhat differently distributed. Both regimes rewarded the farming sector but reduced its independence and political weight to practically nothing. By the late 1930s, the farmers served the war aims of the regimes with none of the influence claimed by industry.

The alliance with large landowners had been fundamental in Italian fascism from its origins. The Fascists adopted two themes that would also be taken up by the Nazis: that rural society was a barrier to radical, alien ideologies and that the nation had to be as self-sufficient in foodstuffs as possible. The additional fact that neither regime was completely certain of its hold over the urban working classes also played a part in the bias toward agriculture. Yet the farming sector continued to lose ground with respect to industry and services, although the process probably took place more slowly than might have been the case if the regimes had not intervened. Between 1921 and 1940 Italian agriculture dropped from 38.3 per cent of national income to 29.8 per cent and farming incomes fell from 66 per cent of non-farming incomes to 36 per cent in 1936. The harsh conditions in rural Italy made it difficult to stem the internal migration to cities and larger towns.

In Italy the chief beneficiaries of Fascist agricultural policies were the large landowners and agri-businesses of the dynamic North. The power of the peasant leagues to threaten the rural *status quo* was permanently eliminated. Fascist peasant labour organizations offered little resistance to the agrarian associations. Laws passed in 1919 that gave some social insurance and unemployment compensation to limited numbers of agricultural workers were repealed. A second benefit came from the major reclamation projects undertaken by the regime after the mid-1920s. Most of the funding went to the North and aided large agri-business groups: sugar beet, rice and wheat producers and manufacturers of farm machinery and fertilizers. Finally the famous Battle for Grain, announced in 1925, and the ruralization campaign of 1927 provided tariff and other incentives for the planting of cereals. Italy made undoubted progress in becoming self-sufficient in these food grains but at the cost of forcing up the price of fodder and harming the livestock industry and to the detriment of export-oriented fruit and vegetable producers. Overall, the Italian agrarian sector remained backward and marked by a slow pace of mechanization. By 1936 only 32,500 tractors and 30,000 threshing machines were being used. Small farming was particularly fragmented and primitive: 83 per cent of private holdings were less than two hectares. The agricultural depression of 1927 drove many small farmers out and led to an increase in sharecropping and tenant farming.[4]

If the initial support for the Fascists in Italy came from large landowners in the Po Valley, the Nazis derived their backing from a massive shift of small-holders to the NSDAP after 1928. In the September 1930 elections the Nazis polled 35 per cent of the vote in communities of under 2000 inhabitants.[5] To a much greater extent than was true in the Fascist regime, the Nazi movement absorbed the biases of the smaller landowners against the great estates of eastern Germany. Once the NSDAP took power, it made several important gestures toward its rural constituencies, but at the expense of the autonomy and real political power of the peasantry. The Nazis quickly ousted the remaining conservatives from the existing agrarian organizations such as the national Landbund and the local agricultural chambers. By the end of 1933 they controlled all rural organizations.

Initially policy was set by the Nationalist Alfred Hugenberg who held the Agriculture Ministry from 30 January to June 1933. Hugenberg stopped foreclosures and eased the burden of debt on small farmers by forcing up prices. Although the situation on the land improved in the first half of the year, Hugenberg's days were numbered. Walter Darré, the ambitious head of the Nazi rural organization, was determined to carve out his sphere within the new Nazi state. On 29 June 1933 Darré became Minister of Agriculture. Two major pieces of legislation then established the Nazi framework for agriculture. A marketing organization, the Reichsnährstand, allowed the state to reorganize the market and to fix prices for agricultural goods. From September 1933 all important agricultural products were subjected to price controls. The scope of the new organization covered everything from farmers to cooperatives and processing industries, but after the economic recovery took hold, the controls acted to keep food cheaper than it might have been under pure market conditions.

The second Nazi initiative for agriculture was the Reich Entailed Farm Law of 29 September 1933. This racial and ruralist law created a kind of land trust for a number of medium-sized farms of peasants who could prove financial stability and pure German blood from 1800. The Entailed Farm Law was too limited to stop the flight of small farmers and landless peasants to the cities; nor did it do anything to ameliorate the harshness of life on the land that made cities more attractive. By the mid-1930s the Nazi regime had created two vast sectoral organizations: Ley's Labour Front and Darré's agricultural organization. Both trespassed on the territorial prerogatives of the Gauleiters but also on each other as they struggled to control the rural labour force and regulate the agricultural markets.

Both regimes passed laws that discouraged flight from the land. The Italians required migrants to cities to obtain residency permits and imposed restrictions on industrial construction in urban areas. The Nazis used shortage in urban housing and legal limitations on mobility to force people to stay on the land. Both governments experimented with internal colonization. The Italians undertook construction of a number of new model towns in Sardinia and in the drained swamp land of central Italy. During the late 1930s projects were formulated for mass peasant migration to newly created villages in Libya. In the end, however, rearmament and war mobilization thwarted the ruralization plans.

8 Autarky and economic mobilization

Martin Broszat has described the relationship of business groups to the Nazi regime in a way that also applied to Fascist Italy after 1935. Private capitalism was not directly challenged; yet the decisions of individual industrial managers and corporate boards were superseded by the military and foreign policy goals of the state. In so far as was possible, this intervention in both Italy and Germany took place in a way that did not interfere in the pursuit of private profit.

> But the increase in private business profits was certainly not the main outcome of National Socialist economic policy. Nor was it the private businessman who was able to thrive in the Third Reich. Instead a type of economic leader was thrown up who was half functionary of the regime and half private businessman.[1]

The Fascist war economy was marked by four features that distinguished it to some degree from the simultaneous Nazi mobilization. First, the regime entrusted management of the state sector and the system of exchange control to the hands of competent but non-party bureaucrats. The result further reinforced the power of the state, not that of the PNF and its affiliates. Second, the new economic system continued to reward already extremely powerful firms who controlled the cartel structure. These cartels were able to secure sufficient foreign exchange for the purchase of raw materials and to take advantage of the opportunities in areas of Fascist military activity. A revolving door for the military–industrial–civil service elite ensured that those who were profiting from the regime would continue to do so. Third, the economic system was increasingly insulated from the world system by managed trade and exchange controls. Finally, the basic decisions regarding the uses to which this war economy was to be put were to be removed from the control of the industrialists, the state managers and the military. The war economy accentuated the administrative confusion that plagued the Fascist style of rule. The breakdown of cabinet responsibility over the economy and over most other aspects of the public administration, coupled with the fragmentation of power in newly created agencies, resulted in what Jane Caplan called 'a pluralism of centralized administrative systems'.[2] A system of 'collective irresponsibility' entrapped the most intelligent participants who found it easier to remain in office, to reap private profit and to execute an increasingly risky foreign policy.

As we have seen, the basic structure of the Fascist economic system was a response to the Great Depression and therefore preceded the changes that marked the shift to a permanent war economy after 1935. The timing is important because it took place when the conservative, stabilizing compromises behind the regime still held. When these same instruments were later used to put the economy on a war footing, they never lost their original conservative character; many were so integrated into the structure of the Italian industrial economy that they eventually became part of the post 1945 mixed economic system. Germany's parastate system was almost exclusively part of the general mobilization for war and perished with the Nazi regime.

With the IRI and the other Depression-inspired moves, the Fascist regime remained faithful to the *étatiste* solutions prevalent throughout interwar Europe. Differences were often matters of degree, not conception, although the elimination of an independent labour movement and the imposition of an authoritarian political structure gave Fascist Italy more administrative latitude. The situation changed with the imposition of economic sanctions by the League of Nations in October 1935. Sanctions accelerated a process initiated earlier in the year when the government introduced tight restrictions on foreign exchange and created the Superintendency of Foreign Exchange and Commerce. Colonial expansion in Africa and the war economy of the late 1930s brought ever closer ties between key industrial sectors and the government for joint ventures in the development of synthetics, projects in the new African empire and military contracts.

In February 1935, Mussolini appointed Felice Guarneri, a manager from the Confederation of Italian Industry, as Head of the Superintendency of Foreign Exchange. Foreign currency was required to be deposited at the Bank of Italy, which then reallocated it for the purchase of raw materials. Guarneri saw to it that the distribution was carried out by the existing cartels, organized for this purpose as corporative boards. By 1936, 75 per cent of production and marketing was done by these cartels under supervision of the Ministry of Corporations. When sanctions were imposed by the League of Nations in October 1935, exchange controls were tightened further. In March of the following year Mussolini officially declared autarky to be national policy.

The German regime pushed ahead much further with state and party direction. Peter Hayes aptly described the general framework:

> All in all, while the regime paid lip-service to property rights, removed much of the risk from private enterprise, and invoked the national welfare, the Nazis also prevented business from arriving at common positions, blocked unsanctioned uses of corporate funds, prevented capital flight, and established administrative procedures for punishing uncooperative employers.[3]

The Nazis made more use of parastate ventures in their planning for war than did the Fascists. Nothing like Hermann Göring's empire existed in Italy. Göring controlled the Four Year Plan, the Reichswerke Hermann Göring, the Airforce and the Prussian administration. What Hitler did for all of Germany, Göring reproduced within his military-industrial complex. Private capitalism still existed, but in Germany, even more than in Italy, it was forced to operate under new rules established by the military ambitions of the regime.

The framework for all Nazi policy was the decision, taken in 1933, to rearm. Thereafter, the debate would be about the pace at which the economy would be militarized. In 1934, Economics Minister Hjalmar Schacht embarked on a programme of economic stimulation, regulated trade, joint ventures for synthetics and primary reliance on private enterprise to achieve the goals set by the military and by Hitler. He envisaged a gradual reintegration of Germany into the international trading and financial system once

Germany achieved full recovery. His plan called for allocation by the state of foreign exchange according to military priorities for heavy industrial production. To overcome credit shortages, government procurement was paid for by bills accepted by a special company, Metallurgischen Forschungs GmbH (Mefo), which had been set up by industry and the government itself. These Mefo bills then circulated as payment for other goods and were used by banks to expand credit.

Autarky was present from the beginning in the form of ventures with private industry for the production of synthetic fuel, textiles and lignite. Trade was regulated by bilateral barter and clearing agreements with various neighbouring states. Domestic private consumption was discouraged, but the government ensured that basic needs in foodstuffs were maintained. To this end, the entire agricultural sector was subjected to intense regulation, initially as a means of supporting farm prices but increasingly to keep food prices down. In July and September 1933 the basic legislation for the Reich Food Estate and for price supports was put into place.

Consensus over economic policy broke down in 1936 with consequences that substantially differentiated the Italian from the German model. Schacht feared overheating an economy that was already reaching full employment and urged a limited version of autarky, a somewhat slower pace of rearmament, and partial reintegration in the international economy. He clashed with Darré, the Agriculture Minister and Head of the Food Estate, over the level of foreign exchange that would be allocated to buy fuel for food production while maintaining the same high level of military rearmament. The dispute led to a significant reorganization of the economic command structure to the disadvantage of Schacht. Hermann Göring was appointed first to a committee to survey the needs of the economy and then to direct the new planning apparatus. With the Four Year Plan of 1936 a turning point was reached. In Richard Overy's words,

> [The ambitions of the Nazis] were integral to Hitler's overall plan to re-shape German society and pursue racial imperialism. The period of compromise gave way to the period of Nazification, not because Hitler had run out of alternatives but because this was the alternative to which his policy had been remorselessly progressing, regardless of circumstance.[4]

The Nazis opted for a more radical policy of autarky and for rearmament without regard for exchange problems, raw materials and labour shortages and inflationary pressures. In Germany, 1936 marked a decisive shift away from traditional institutions of government. The Economics Ministry was superseded by the bureaucracy of the Four Year Plan and then, in 1938, placed in the hands of Walter Funk who was completely under Göring's thumb. Schacht's other power base, the Reichsbank, was also diminished when Göring secured control of the Dresdner Bank and used it for the operations of the Four Year Plan.

If the Schachtian model resembled the Italian system and both regimes adopted autarky without regard for foreign exchange and raw materials problems, Göring's power over the economy had no counterpart in the Fascist state in the way it fundamentally rearranged earlier compromises. Initially, the Nazi movement eschewed direct state ownership. Several of the banks that fell under state control during the early part of the depression were restored to private ownership between 1933 and 1937. All of this changed with the Four Year Plan. In 1937 Göring overrode resistance from industrialists to his project to exploit low-grade, high-cost iron ore in central and southern Germany. He then built a new steel plant, the Reichswerke Hermann Göring; this had matastasized into the largest industrial firm in Europe by the outbreak of the Second World War. The Reichswerke HG was involved in manufacturing processes that ranged from coal production, manufacture of heavy machinery and production of synthetic fuels to transport, construction and food processing. This state–private enterprise differed from the IRI, which also controlled significant portions of the steel, shipbuilding and shipping industries. The IRI did not operate in opposition to existing private capital. Göring's Four Year Plan and the Reichswerke HG sought to restructure and subordinate the entire German private sector and, from 1938 onward, to pillage large parts of the occupied territories. His Four Year Plan operation had special divisions for iron, steel, the machine industry, oil, textiles and automobiles. The construction division under Fritz Todt became a huge enterprise in its own right. But it should be noted once again that favoured private enterprise like FIAT in Italy or IG Farben (which saw a 70 per cent increase in profits) and Daimler Benz in Germany could do quite well under this system.

9 The new 'fascist' community
Demography and race

Traditionally, a clear distinction had been made between nazism and fascism on matters of race. This was a position that I held as I worked on the first edition of this book. Since 1995 a number of works have made me reconsider earlier assumptions.[1]

Both Fascist Italy and Nazi Germany proposed the formation of new national communities that were based on three principles: the glorification of the ethnic group over all other peoples, the adoption of measures to protect the health of the ethnic group and the necessity to exclude elements deemed incompatible with the health of the national community. Both regimes believed that the racial or ethnic nation was a kind of organism that needed to expand to flourish. The Fascists and the Nazis were convinced that peoples were divided into inferior and superior races and that the stronger and more dynamic peoples had the right to expand against the weaker. Both regimes had a deep hostility to their Slavic neighbours – Poles, Czechs and Russians in the case of Nazi Germany; Slovenes, Croats and Serbs in the case of Italy. Each regime was fueled by anger. Germany resented the restrictions imposed by the Versailles Treaty of 1919 and Italy felt that it had been treated badly by the other victors at the Paris Peace Conference, but this bitterness went beyond politics. Italy was not respected because it was not strong. Italians were viewed as mere 'mandolin players' in Mussolini's words. Only when Italy and Germany were powerful would they be respected and feared. Obviously, neither regime accepted the idea of a common humanity that gave all peoples certain rights. As Hannah Arendt argued in her *Origins of Totalitarianism*, the rights of man became restricted to the main ethnic community and those outside, or minorities inside, no longer shared in these rights, thereby assuming a diminished status as humans.[2] This proposition, obvious from the start in Nazi Germany, was initally not as clear in Fascist Italy. In Italy during the 1920s political enemies like socialists, communists and democrats were targeted; also from the beginning the regime revealed a contempt for the Slavic minorities on Italy's northeastern border with Yugoslavia. The Fascists began to apply policies of exclusion from the national community more broadly with the imposition of racial legislation after the creation of the Italian empire in 1936.

The new national community promoted positive and negative measures to protect national health. The Fascist *popolo* and the Nazi *Volksgemeinschaft* aimed at fashioning a new type of humanity. Each regime envisaged a massive project of re-education of the national culture that would involve medicine, biology and the social sciences. All aspects of modern technology were to be mobilized to advance the health of the national community. Each regime relied on academically trained experts and civil servants to realize the vision of reshaping the national community. Central to this mission of re-education was the obliteration of the distinction between the public and private spheres. In the 'fascist' totalitarian conception of the state no separation of the public from the private could be tolerated. Obviously, regimes that were based from the outset on a compromise with established social and economic elites faced institutional limitations on how far they could go in imposing new values on the national community. Insofar as the compromises held, and they did to a greater degree in Italy, areas of private life and civil society remained beyond the reach of the state. The overall aim of each regime was to educate the people to accept the new value system and to reject older cultural norms.

Demography

Both regimes used many of the same positive measures to encourage large families: tax benefits, preferences to married men in state employment, rules to force women from the employment market, allotments for children and grants to married couples. But both regimes faced social and demographic realities that worked against a draconian application of laws limiting the possibilities open to women. In Italy, even before the First World War, more women than men were in the 15- to 21-year cohort, and roughly one-third of all women worked, mainly in agriculture. Male war casualties left far more women in the active population in both countries after 1919. For example, in Germany, the excess of women before the First World War was 800,000 but reached 2.8 million after 1919.[3] Increasing numbers of women would never marry and would have to attend school or enter the workforce. The expanding service sector in both countries drew women into secretarial ranks or as telephone or telegraphy operators. By 1932, German women comprised one-third of the workforce with 11.5 million females employed. Italian economic backwardness and chronic unemployment allowed Fascist Italy to take a much harder line even after the early 1930s when the Nazi regime had begun to come to terms with the need for female labour. As Victoria De Grazia put it,

> Fascist policies toward working women thus seem less drastic than those of Nazi Germany which in 1934 expelled women outright from state employment. Yet Italian female labor participation was lower at the start and occupied less qualified positions than in Germany. The combination of customary biases and new discriminations, operating in an economy where jobs were hard to find anyway and where the state picked up the slack by acting as employers of last resort, made Fascist Italy a uniquely hostile environment for the employment of women.[4]

Although the Fascist movement initially saw itself as an elite that stressed quality over quantity, this position changed dramatically in favour of increasing the birth-rate in the mid-1920s. In December 1925 the Opera Nazionale Maternità ed Infanzia (ONMI) was created to reduce the high rate of infant mortality. The ONMI soon merged into a larger campaign to increase the birth rate. The Duce was influenced by the demographer-statistician Corrado Gini who believed that number was power and that young people were naturally expansive. Gini argued that there was no optimum population, nor did he mind that population density would lower the standard of living. Hardship would simply toughen a people. Gini also believed that authoritarian governments were the only ones that could coerce a people to reshape its population. In July 1926 Gini was put in charge of the Italian Central Statistical Office (ISTAT). This scientist and technocrat had access to the Duce on an almost monthly basis. On 27 May 1927 Mussolini announced a new 'battle' to increase the birthrate to 60 million by the second half of the century. In a 1928 article, 'Number as Force', published in *Il Popolo d'Italia* and then as an introduction to a book by the future Nazi SS official, Richard Korherr, Mussolini linked the decline of civilization to a falling birthrate and predicted a future racial conflict between white and non-white races.

In 1926, the Fascist regime launched a full-scale demographic battle. Penalties for abortion and for dissemination of birth control information and devices were imposed. In 1926 a tax on bachelors was introduced to help fund the ONMI and unmarried individuals were denied preference in the state bureaucracy.[5] A 1928 law gave limited tax benefits to large families (state employees had to have seven children and other workers ten). Promotions also favoured married males with children. Welfare rules were rewritten to keep women out of the workforce. In 1934 a National Workers Fund for Family Allowances was established with only breadwinners able to qualify for assistance. The head of the family had to be a male, unless the woman was widowed, separated or married to a disabled husband. In 1935 a Day of the Mother and Child was introduced and the Fascists took up the Nazi idea of marriage loans. Unfortunately, aid in the various programmes was so meagre that it did not cover the cost of additional children.

Nazi population policy mixed positive and negative incentives much more aggressively than in Italy. On the positive side a marriage loan programme was begun in 1933. The regime also began construction of housing, but demand far outstripped supply. Grants were made for the purchase of furniture and other household items to families with four or more children. Former communists or socialists or those deemed otherwise asocial would be unable to qualify for many of these benefits and a medical examination was required for those receiving marriage loans. As in Italy birth control centres were shut down. In 1936 Police Chief and SS leader Heinrich Himmler set up an office to combat both homosexuality and abortion. The Nazis created their own equivalent of the ONMI in 1934 with the NS Volkswohlfärht (NSV) and the Hilfs-werke Mutter und Kind in 1934. Centres were set up to advise mothers and children but the focus was on the need to increase the population.

Negative measures were present from the start in Nazi Germany. The Law for the Prevention of Hereditarily Diseased Offspring of 14 July 1933 introduced compulsory sterilization for those with certain diseases. Between 1933 and 1939, 320,000 sterilizations took place; nothing even remotely comparable occurred in Italy. On 18 October 1935 with the Law for the Protection of the Hereditary Health of the German People or the Marriage Health Law, prospective couples were required to have a certificate of fitness to marry. In the 1938 Marriage Law restrictions on divorce were eased with new grounds such as refusal to procreate or merely living apart for three years – again, something impossible in Catholic Italy.

Racial policy

The Nazi regime adopted policies to exclude certain groups on racial grounds from the new 'people's community'. Most directly, this applied to Jews but it was also extended to Gypsies and Slavic peoples who were deemed racially inferior. Fascist Italy adopted no clear racial criteria for membership in the national community until 1936. From 1922 until the mid-1930s the Italian regime seemed to reject the biological racial theories that were the basis for Nazi policy. Yet in the late 1930s the two regimes began to converge, at least in legislation, on issues of race. The shift in both countries represented a step forward in the totalitarian project to remake society. Fascist racism was not a simple imitation of what was going on in Nazi Germany or the result of the political alliance between the two regimes after 1936, but rather something more sweeping and more complex.

In 1933, the Jewish population of Germany was about 500,000 out of a total population of roughly 70 million. Most German Jews lived in large cities and about half the population was concentrated in Berlin, Franfurt-am-Main, Breslau, Hamburg, Cologne and Leipzig. Few Jews lived in the smaller provincial centres or in small towns. Most were employed in trade and commerce (63 per cent); close to 13 per cent of those employed were in the professions and state and private white collar positions. The Nazis were determined to exclude these German Jews from any presence in the larger Germany society. The process of exclusion evolved in three stages from 1933 to the outbreak of the war.

The Nazi seizure of power on 30 January 1933 sparked a wave of violence by the SA against Jewish-owned shops, department stores, and individuals. It culminated in the relatively unsuccessful boycott of Jewish businesses on 1 April 1933. The negative domestic and foreign reaction to this lawlessness led Hitler to pull back the SA and a two year process of legislating separation began. After protests by Berlin lawyers against the presence of Jews in March 1933, the Prussian commissioner Hans Kerrl set limits on the number of Jewish jurists. Jews, Socialists and Communists lost rights as public defenders. Similar purges took place in the other professional organizations. The 7 April Law for the Restoration of the Public Service allowed for a broader purge of public employment, including the schools and universities. In May all non-Aryan public employees were dismissed. The number of Jewish university students dropped from 3,950 in 1933 to 548 in 1934–5. Unofficial boycotts were the rule. Aryan doctors tried to force out the roughly 9,000 Jewish doctors. By 1934 only 6,000 were still practicing.

The next stage came in the summer and autumn of 1935. Legislation was preceded by another wave of SA violence during the summer. Then, on 15 September at the Nazi party congress, Hitler announced the Nuremberg Laws. The announcement of new legislation and the regulations that followed marked a decisive step in the creation of a race state. The Reich Citizenship Law made Aryan status a requirement for membership in the national community. The Law for the Protection of German Blood prohibited marriages between Jews and Aryans. However, as Claudia Koonz had recently pointed out, the Nazis found themselves in a dilemma. The initial idea was to base Jewishness on biological markers. Using the widest measure, some 800,000 people could be defined as Jewish or part Jewish. The Reich statistical office came up with a figure of 550,000 full Jews, 200,000 half-Jews, and 100,000 quarter Jews. Nazi hardliners wanted to base Jewishness on only one full Jewish grandparent; others felt that three or four were necessary. Koonz notes that every bureaucrat had his own measure. Even the question of marriage was vexing. In 1933 of the 15 million existing marriages, only 35,000 were mixed.[6] Hitler's 15 September speech did not mention biology, nor did it propose a definition of a Jew. The Führer opted for the mildest of the three versions put before him; in November, the legal experts issued regulations that applied the laws to those with three or four Jewish grandparents. A German with a single Jewish grandparent who did not practice the Jewish religion would be considered an Aryan.[7]

The Nuremberg legislation had two consequences. As Koonz points out, anti-Semitism shifted from the streets into offices, neighbourhoods and private life. The process of Aryanizing businesses picked up. Jews could no longer collect debts owed them. But after 1935 the Nazis realized that biological markers for determining a Jew were inadequate:

> No blood type, odor, foot- or fingerprint pattern, skull size, ear lobe or nose shape, or any other physiological marker of Jewishness withstood scrutiny . . . From that point on, cultural stereotypes about Jewish character displaced physical traits in the hunt for sources of Jewishness, and the burden of proof shifted away from the natural sciences to the social sciences and the humanities.[8]

In short, it became a question of finding a Jewish mentality and character.

The campaign against Jewish influence passed to the universities, newly created specialized cultural institutes, the police, and the SS. As Götz Aly put it,

> . . . the Nazi regime relied to an exceptional degree upon academically trained advisers and that it made use of their skills. Their ideas were transmitted upwards to the highest echelons by civil servants, especially by the secretaries of state attached to the various ministries, many of whom belonged to the General Council of the Four Year Plan agency in which capacity they ranked higher than their own ministers.[9]

The final stage of Nazi policy came after the Kristallnacht of 9 November 1939 when Nazi thugs went on a rampage that destroyed remaining Jewish businesses, synagogues and private homes. This violence was followed by new restrictions that limited the rights of Jews to the point of total exclusion. Between 1938 and 1942 the regulations piled up one after another. Finally, in 1942, the diarist Victor Klemperer listed them:

1) To be home after eight or nine in the evening. Inspection!
2) Expelled from one's own house.
3) Ban on radio, ban on telephone.
4) Ban on theaters, cinemas, museums.
5) Ban on subscribing to or purchasing periodicals.
6) Ban on using public transport: three phases: a) buses banned, only front platform of tram permitted, b) all use banned, except to work, c) to work on foot, unless one lives 2½ miles away or is sick (but it is hard to get a doctor's certificate). Also ban on taxicabs [. . .]
8) Ban on purchasing cigars or any kind of smoking materials.
9) Ban on purchasing flowers. [. . .]
11) Ban on going to the barber [. . .]
13) Compulsory surrender of typewriters,
14) of furs and woollen blankets,
15) of bicycles . . . ,
16) of deck chairs,
17) of dogs, cats, birds . . .

In September 1941 Klemperer noted that Jews were forced to wear yellow identification stars. Even earlier, they had to take the names Sara and Israel.[10]

Racism in Italy

Fascist Italy adopted no racial laws until 1936. Most Italian scientists rejected German biologically based theories of race. Some of the most prominent, Corrado Gini for one, felt that Italy was the product of a creative mixture of peoples. Another noted scientist, Nicola Pende, rejected the idea of pure races. Nor did Aryanism have an easy time in Italy where theories of Mediterranean racial types were much more congenial. Finally, Italian science tended to weigh environmental factors more heavily than heredity. One great exception to the rejection of biological racism existed. As Roberto Maiocchi put it:

> Biology-based racism, almost always rejected in theory, manifested itself concretely in practice when it came to analyze people of color, blacks in particular. In the books of our Africanists, but also in literary works, the image of black races

as inferior races was taken for granted. In Italy of the 1930s, almost no one proposed that the blacks were not morally and intellectually inferior to whites.[11]

But Italian colonial policies were no more racist than those of other powers and Italy's excesses, such as the elimination of over a quarter of the population of Libyan Cyranaica in the early 1930s, did not differ radically from imperialist practices elsewhere. It was still possible as late as the 1933 organic laws for Somalia and Eritrea for mixed-race children of unknown parents to gain Italian citizenship.

The decisive turn came between 1936 and 1938, many Fascists, including Mussolini, feared that the Fascist revolution had stalled. Unlike the Nazis who had recently taken power, the Fascists had ruled for over a decade and the regime was mired in the compromises that had been made with traditional power centres from 1925 to the early 1930s. Moreover, with the conquest of Ethiopia in early 1936 the Fascists had the opportunity to create an entirely new society in the 'empty' space of East Africa. The regime envisaged major colonization projects in Ethiopia and Libya that would vastly increase the Italian population in Africa. Therefore, an imperial policy meant also a racial policy that would define relations with the subject peoples. The racial legislation for the empire of 1937 ended the possibility that black Africans could ever be citizens. They would remain permanent subjects of Italy. For the first time biologically-based exclusion was written into law. Eventually, in 1939 a new crime, damage to the prestige of the race, was created. Prison terms were imposed for long-term sexual relations with Africans, mixed-race children were relegated to the status of Africans, and legal recognition of these children or the granting of citizenship was forbidden. The adoption of racism in the empire came not from any settler community but was dictated by and intimately connected with developments at home.

Racial criteria, introduced in 1937, became generalized in Fascist Italy within a year. As with the Nuremberg Laws of 1935, the Fascist racial laws in 1938 were part of an effort to regulate personal behavior. As the historian Gabriele Turi put it,

> The racial policy of which the anti-Semitic persecution is a part, belongs to the totalitarian logic of the Fascist state which

sought to recover through violence that hit directly at the Jews but constituted a warning to everyone, a consensus that it felt weakening in the world of culture and in the middle classes.[12]

The Fascist regime decreed new language regulations that substituted *lei* with *voi* as the form of address; the handshake was replaced with the Fascist salute; increasingly uniforms were required for civil servants. In this context, the racial laws were yet another means not only of re-educating Italians, but also of showing that no area of culture or social life was safe from the power of the state.

The crucial year, 1938, began with a series of measures that foreshadowed the wholesale adoption of official racism. In February, the Ministry of National Education asked for a census of Jewish students in the universities. Similar measures were taken to ascertain the number of Jewish military officers and the number of Jewish civil servants in the Interior ministry. In March, Italy closed its borders to Jewish refugees from Austria and began to ask for religious backgrounds of foreigners who requested to study in Italian universities. In July, a number of scientists, headed by the obscure Guido Landra, published the Manifesto of Racial Scientists. The principles set forth in the document were dictated directly by Mussolini and declared the existence of a pure Aryan Italian race to which Jews did not belong because racial types were biologically determined. A new agency, the General Directorate for Demography and Race (Demorazza), was created and the semi-official newspaper, *La Difesa della Razza*, was launched in August. As in Nazi Germany, restrictions piled up to enforce separation. A ban on foreign Jewish enrollment in Italian universities was instituted, which was especially painful because many Jewish students came from countries like Romania or Hungary where quotas on Jewish enrollment had already been imposed; texts by Jewish authors were eliminated, eventually to be extended backward to books published after 1850.[13] Most ominously, a racial census was undertaken on 22 August. In 1943, the Nazi occupiers would come into possession of this and other registers of the Jewish population.

Between September and November 1938 the Fascist regime moved aggressively to positions taken earlier by the Nazi regime as Jews were legally separated from the rest of the population. Mussolini considered revoking the citizenship of all Italian Jews, but restricted application only to those who received citizenship after 1918. The practical impact of the laws and regulations of 1938 excluded Italian Jews from the rights of citizenship and put them into a category very similar to the German Jews after Nuremberg. Africans had already been classed as subjects with no rights to citizenship. Marriage between Italian Aryans and members of other races were forbidden. Jews were expelled from every level of teaching and from all cultural and scientific societies and from the Fascist Party and in December from the military and the entire public administration. In fact, Goebbels complained in November 1938 that Jews could still go to schools with Germans, whereas the Italians closed this option on 5 September.[14] As the historian Enzo Collotti noted, the laws were often less harsh in practice. New Jewish businesses were banned, but old ones, even with fewer customers, were allowed to continue. Closure demanded a bureaucratic decision that was often not forthcoming. But, Collotti cautioned, the humiliation and isolation were real: 'Today one contends that the Italian population did not respect the racial laws, but in reality it [the Italian people] isolated the Jews and therefore in its fashion consented to the application. Even if today, one prefers not to remember it.'[15]

The racial census of August 1938 revealed that Italy had slightly over 58,000 residents who were born to one Jewish parent. Roughly 48,000 were Italian and 10,000 were foreign residents, but only 46,656 were registered in the Jewish community (37,241 Italians and 9,415 foreigners).[16] The Italians found themselves essentially dealing with the same problems that the Nazis faced at the time of the Nuremberg laws: how is Jewishness to be defined? Inevitably, the answer became complicated. The child of two Jewish parents was always Jewish, even if non-religious. The child of two Aryans was always Aryan, even if converted to Judaism. A child of an unknown father simply followed the classification of the mother. As in Nazi Germany three Jewish grandparents automatically consigned one to the status of a Jew; one or two Jewish grandparents could go either way, but for the child to be Aryan with two Jewish grandparents, each of the two grandparents had to be in a racially mixed marriage. In the cases of one Jewish grandparent, it was important that the mixed parent not practice the Jewish religion. The Italian laws also involved procedures for Aryanization and reclassification.[17]

Mussolini backed away from the biological racism of the Racial Manifesto in 1939, but so-called spiritual-cultural and biological racism co-existed uncomfortably in Italy. Perhaps this distinction is irrelevant. In the end, both German and Italian racial policies excluded certain groups of people from membership in the national community on the basis of both blood and incompatibility of culture or mentality or spiritual qualities.

The crucial difference between the two regimes was in the execution of their racial policies. Hitler and Mussolini set the overall racial goals, but only in Germany did these policies enjoy broad support in the Nazi party and the bureaucracy. Such was not the case in Italy. To borrow a phrase from Ian Kershaw, very few Italians were 'working toward the Duce' on matters of race and anti-Semitism. Italians somehow failed to understand why a minority group numbering fewer than 50,000 could be a threat. The absence of enthusiasm in the state and party apparatus mirrored the larger society's reluctance to develop a 'racial consciousness'. If few Italians showed much open solidarity with the beleaguered Jewish community, not many wanted to follow Nazi Germany on the road to the Holocaust.

10 The new community
Women and youth

Women

The fascist position had always been that class distinctions were artificial and superficial but that biologically determined gender roles were immutable. Thus both the Fascist and Nazi regimes sought to transcend class distinctions within the national or racial community, while dividing society firmly along gender lines.

Policy on gender arose in part out of the overwhelmingly male composition of the movements. After 1920, Italian fascism responded to the pressure from veterans to eliminate female competition from the workforce. From 1929 to 1933 the Nazis did not so much act in favour of veterans as they did all unemployed males who were hit by the Great Depression. On taking power, they had only to continue existing legislation, passed in May 1932, which allowed the dismissal of economically secure, married female civil servants, so-called double dippers.[1] The Nazis limited the right of appeal, raised the age at which permanent civil service status might be granted, and cut the amount of severance pay.

Pragmatism and electoral considerations are not sufficient to explain policy toward women. Fascist and Nazi populism had a profoundly anti-egalitarian core. The two movements had been scathing in their attacks on the levelling aspirations of the Marxist parties. Rhetoric about 'people's communities' aside, both regimes mistrusted and feared the urban blue-collar worker.[2] Their hierarchical vision of society did not fundamentally challenge the existing social order. Uncontrolled social mobility was certainly discouraged. In this context, women played a key stabilizing role. Perry Willson's description of the situation in Italy might apply equally to Nazi Germany:

Fascism, for all its rhetoric about the end of class conflict, mobilized women in a manner that quite clearly reinforced rather than diminished class divisions. It was, of course, a core role of the *donne fasciste* to make class 'co-operation' appear to function for, in much propaganda, it was their work which was primarily featured in lists of the 'achievements of the regime'. Their activities, such as the running of children's holiday camps, the provision of facilities for poor mothers, and so on, was supposed to 'spread the feeling that the Party is watching over and interested and concerned with the living conditions of humble people so that, as far as possible, their poverty and discomfort can be alleviated'.[3]

Large families perpetuated older models of lower class subservience and dependency. In regimes that discouraged domestic consumption, Fascist and Nazi populism during the 1930s attacked the lifestyle of the bourgeoisie for its hedonism, decadence and individualism. Most pointedly, the modern woman, freed from family obligations and working outside the home, symbolized everything that was wrong with the 'self-centreed' middle-class outlook.[4] Through school texts, magazines and film, the rural family was proclaimed as the ideal. By glorifying the peasant housewife, the regimes could make a safe, non-subversive, populist appeal to the generic *popolo* or *Volk*. Thus the battle against feminism and sexual equality dovetailed with the anti-urban, anti-consumerist, reactionary side of both movements.[5]

The exclusion of women from the workplace operated differently for peasant and blue-collar workers and for white-collar or professional positions. In Italy most working women had traditionally been employed in agriculture. As late as 1921, just over half of all working women were in the agricultural sector where they comprised 44.7 per cent of the entire farm workforce. That same year 39 per cent of those employed in industry were female workers. These figures declined only slightly during the Fascst era: 34.4 per cent of all workers in industrial employment in 1931 and 33.1 per cent in 1936 were women. In the Fascist agricultural unions there were almost 560,000 women and slightly under 1.4 million males but the vast majority of the women were ill-paid, short contract, seasonal or day laborers. The overall shift in the economy from agriculture and textile production played more of a role in reducing female employment than did Fascist policy. In so far as it affected the balance, the Fascist regime used wage cuts to make male workers more competitive and a series of maternity benefits and other restrictions to render female labour more expensive and complicated for employers. As salaries were compressed, workers were paid partly in the form of family allotments and marriage and housing loans, which often required that the woman leave the workforce.

Restrictions on female professional employment were more direct. Fascist legislation of the 1920s excluded females from the teaching of history, philosophy and classical languages. During the early 1930s women were no longer admitted to certain examinations for state employment. Finally, in 1938, a 10 per cent quota was set on all female employment in both the public administration and large and medium-sized private firms, except for categories deemed predominantly female. Only in 1940 did this policy of exclusion collpase under the pressure of wartime mobilization.

In Germany, pressure from male civil servants even before the advent of the Nazi regime forced restrictions on women in public service. A restrictive law was passed in May 1932, which was carried over by the Nazis. The marriage loan programme until 1937 required that women stop working upon marriage. The easing of restrictions probably accounted for the fact that by 1939, over 40 per cent of all marriages in Nazi Germany involved these loans.

By 1939, with 37 per cent of the German workforce comprised of women, the regime had used up the voluntary female labour market. At the outbreak of the Second World War, 14.6 million women were working. This was 50 per cent more than in the depression year of 1933, but they were concentrated in the consumer goods industry, not in industrial employment. In 1939, a compulsory women's labour service was introduced to make up for labour shortages in agriculture. The schools in both Germany and Italy also introduced a mandatory labour service. Despite the demands to tap these sources of female labour, the number of working women only rose by 300,000 by 1944. Nazi labour organizations and the compulsory labour service could not overcome Hitler's reluctance to draw in more women. In fact, he went to great lengths to keep wives of soldiers at home so as not to disturb the morale of the troops. The American and British liberal democratic regimes were able to mobilize women for the war effort far more effectively than did either the Nazi or Fascist regimes. The Nazi compulsory labour service law seems merely to have forced young women into marriage because service was not compulsory for married women.

Although education became a necessity for both sexes, the Fascist and Nazi regimes, as part of their programme of controlling social mobility and of easing unemployment in overcrowded professions, tried to cut down on the total number of university students. The Fascist educational reform of 1923, like the later Nazi reforms, sought to limit access to higher education, but by the mid-1920s pressure from middle-class families forced the numbers up again for both sexes. Before 1914 only 6 per cent of the university students were female, but by 1928 the figure was 13 per cent. By 1938 women received one-fifth of the degrees awarded in higher education.[6]

The Nazis also capped the growth of German universities to such a degree that by the late 1930s the regime faced shortages in technical professions and a serious crisis in teaching after the initial dismissal of thousands of female teachers. University attendance for both males and females continued to decline into the late 1930s from 60,148 in 1936 to 41,069 in 1938, or less than two-fifths of the 1931 peak.[7] In 1932 almost 19 per cent of the students enrolled in German universities were female; in 1934 women still comprised 12.4 per cent and, despite a cap of 10 per cent on female enrollment, by 1939 they had climbed back up to 20 per cent and reached 30 per cent as male students were mobilized for war service. But female students and professionals worked under many restrictions. All female school supervisors were ousted and 60 per cent of the teacher training faculty was fired. Women's institutions were not to teach Latin for the first five years and no science was allowed for the final three.[8] In professional fields, the few female lawyers and judicial officers were hit hard but Nazi policy actually created increased demand for women in some professions, such as medicine where the need for expanded services for mothers and children opened opportunities for doctors and nurses.

In the end, neither regime dared close higher education completely to women, although the Nazis tried to direct them into courses of study such as home economics and modern languages, which made it difficult to enter most university faculties. The Fascist School Charter of 1939 reformed the female institutes with a similar purpose in mind. Few women chose these options; they tended in practice to concentrate in the already overcrowded faculties of letters, teaching institutes and certain professions such as pharmacy. The freedom allowed to women was a concession to the middle and lower middle-class constituency of fascism and nazism that could not afford to see its children excluded from educational opportunities.

Women were no exception to the fascist practice of granting some autonomy within limited spheres. Organizations for a women's world with its own hierarchies and leadership principle existed on three levels: first, those concerned with motherhood and the rearing of children; second, organizations that dealt with working women; and third, the more strictly political organizations. Although all three types existed in other countries, the authoritarian, anti-pluralistic and hierarchical features again distinguished the Fascist and Nazi organizations.

In 1925 the Italian Fascist regime created the Opera Nazionale Maternità ed Infanzia (ONMI), one of the many Fascist organizations that survived into the postwar era. The ONMI combined social welfare with the realization of the regime's demographic aims. It sought to block abortion, to provide medical care and, if possible, to involve the fathers of illegitimate children. The entire operation was plagued by an authoritarian structure and never lost its aura of patronizing beneficence. Volunteers were often middle-class women who had little in common with the people they were trying to help. However, the Fascists understood that the high infant death rate was a major and preventable depressant on population growth. The rate of infant mortality did decline, this being attributable in part to the policies of the regime but also to a long-term rise in the standard of living and health care that had been initiated before fascism.

The Nazi mother and child section of the Nazi Welfare Organization (NSV) took on similar tasks. Courses for women on infant care, general health and home economics were attended by about 2 million women by 1940. The Nazis achieved an increase in the birth rate over the depression years of 1929 to 1933, but not a return to nineteenth-century demographic levels or even to those under Weimar.

The Fascist regime, like its Nazi counterpart, did its best to honour large families. In 1933 the regime officially sponsored a Day of the Mother and Child and monetary awards were given to large families in a public ceremony. In addition to creating an official Mother's Day, the Nazis presented medals, such as the Honour Cross of the German Mother, to mothers of numerous children: a bronze for five, silver for six and gold for seven.

Both regimes also sponsored women's sections of the labour organizations. These bodies were ineffective in the struggle to protect the economic status of the female worker but, as Victoria De Grazia pointed out, the regime preferred to treat women workers primarily as females and family members rather than as members of the workforce in order to blur consciousness and cause women to think of themselves as incidental to the active economy.[9] The Massaie Rurali, an affiliate of the PNF with a membership of 850,000 by 1939, organized peasant housewives. The Fascist Confederation of Industrial Workers and the PNF sponsored an organization for female factory and home workers. But neither could engage in collective bargaining and both became social welfare organizations, staffed by party members.

More important for our purposes are the overtly political organizations. Fascist and Nazi women's affiliates served to mobilize women behind the political causes dear to the regimes, to provide cadres for the various social welfare projects and to offer limited leadership roles for committed women whose participation in public life was otherwise restricted. The leader of the National Socialist Womanhood (NSF) organization, Gertrud Scholtz-Klink, controlled an organization of 2.3 million members by 1938. The other, less political mass organization for women, the Deutsche Frauenwerke (DFW), reached 4 million. Comparable Italian organizations were much smaller, The Fasci Femminili had only 600,000 members in 1936 and the total number of organized women was half that of Nazi Germany.[10]

Both Nazi and Fascist women's organizations succeeded best in reaching middle-class women. Neither had much luck in bringing women workers into the movement. But pre-Fascist Italy never had the large political feminist movement that existed in Germany. The Fascists were also more constrained by religion and traditional morality and more dependent on the Church to carry out their demographic and ruralist schemes. Their dependence on the Church during the 1930s meant abandoning much of Catholic rural Italy to the nuns and priests who continued to set public and private standards in Catholic areas. The Fascists were also limited by concessions made to the Church in matters of divorce. Even Fascist racial policy had a fundamentally conservative base. The National Socialists were constrained only in matters that dealt directly with the religious sphere. The Nazis (and to some extent the Fascists as well) were thwarted by conditions of their own making, namely the war effort and economic mobilization. The conservative and stabilizing elements of Nazi ideology – to keep women in their place and maintain them as a pillar of the traditional, hierarchical society could not be reconciled with the political, social and racial ambitions of the regime.

Youth organizations

The Nazi and Fascist parties were to serve as the nucleus of the new political class. But within a few years after taking power it was clear that this was not going to happen with the existing PNF or NSDAP. Both movements suffered from a similar marginalization as initiators of policy. Fascist and Nazi leaders blamed the lethargy and ossification of party cadres on the bourgeois ideals of individualism and self-interest, which had corrupted the education of the older generation.

The sluggishness of the party apparatus, as well as the defects of the larger society, could only be overcome by forming a new, entirely Fascist or Nazi generation. The effort was made on two levels: (1) through mass youth organization to indoctrinate boys and girls in the ideals of the regime, and (2) by more specialized elite education for university students and party cadres. The results of schools for party cadres were disappointing in both regimes, possibly because of lack of time in the case of Nazi Germany. The German Ministry of Education established National Political Schools in 1933, modelled after the military boarding schools, but the idea never took off. More successful were the Adolf Hitler Schools sponsored by von Schirach's Hitler Youth and by Robert Ley's Labour Front. The National Political Schools were to train the new Nazi civil servant; the Adolf Hitler Schools aimed at producing Nazi political leaders. In addition, seven cadre schools (Ordensburgen) were established in picturesque castles for a selected racial elite.

The Italians attempted several variations on the same theme. The School of Fascist Mysticism was founded in 1931 by Mussolini's brother Arnaldo in honour of his recently deceased son. Its aims were to promote the cult of the Duce and to create a class of dedicated militants. Eventually the school ran short courses targeted at teachers and secondary school students, as well as competitions along various propaganda themes. A second initiative was a programme of courses in political preparation, sponsored by the PNF for young party cadres.

In both regimes the experiment in training a political elite failed. The schools merely existed alongside the regular educational system and offered no alternative track. The prestige of the state schools remained unbroken. Moreover, the party schools did not even ensure their graduates a successful placement in a future career because they were too often associated with one set of leaders and mistrusted by the others.

The mass organizations were designed to achieve three aims: (1) to inculcate in the young the basic myths of the regime (cult of the Duce or Führer, national and racial feelings and acceptance of war and violence); (2) to counteract powerful traditional institutions such as the family and churches by alternative models of socialization, and (3) to provide a degree of physical and paramilitary training, sometimes disguised as sport, sometimes not. To this end, the regimes broke down provincial barriers by bringing together young people from all over the country at regional and national meetings in a conscious effort to promote loyalty to the new political system and to forge a single national consciousness.

The results were mixed in Fascist Italy where the ability of the regime to achieve its goals was restricted by the existing spheres of control. The family structure was left unaltered by the government. In Catholic rural Italy the power and authority of the clergy – both male and female – maintained an alternative hierarchy that, while not in conflict with the Fascist order, was separate from it.

The Fascists undertook the systematic organization of young people with the creation of the Opera Nazionale Balilla (ONB) in April 1926. Males aged between 8 and 14 years joined the Balilla and then passed on to the Avanguardisti from the age of 15 to 18 years. Girls were organized into the Piccole Italiane (8 to 12 years) and then in the Giovani Italiane (13 to 18 years). Both male and female organizations began as party organizations, then in 1929 were put under the supervision of the Ministry of National Education. For youths aged over 18 there were the Gruppi Universitari Fascisti (GUF) and in 1930 the Fasci Giovanili di Combattimento for those who did not attend the universities. Interaction between the schools and the ONB was most effective on the elementary level where many of the teachers were also ONB leaders. With the purge of the elementary and secondary schools during the mid-1920s, a compulsory oath of loyalty after 1929 and PNF membership requirements after 1933 for primary and secondary school teachers, the educational institutions were coordinated.

The GUF and the Fasci Giovanili were to be the source of leadership in the party and were not initially part of the ONB. The complexity of this organizational structure led to conflict between leaders of the ONB and PNF organizations and between the Education Ministry and the Fascist Party. Finally, in 1937 Mussolini set up a single youth organization, the Gioventù Italiana del Littorio (GIL), under the secretaryship of the PNF. The GIL had control over the entire youth movement with the exception of the GUF, which was directly responsible to the PNF secretary. By 1938, 99 per cent of secondary school students were theoretically enrolled in the Fascist youth organizations, but membership figures dropped off as larger numbers of teenage youths left school. For example, in 1936, 74 per cent of males were in the Balilla but only 53 per cent were in the Giovani Fascisti (18 to 21 years); 66 per cent of girls were in the Piccole italiani but only 14.8 per cent in the Giovani Fasciste (8 to 14 years). Reflecting the administrative and bureaucratic weakness of the Italian state itself, wide regional variations existed, with membership at its weakest in the South and central Italy.[11]

The Fascist Party leadership, like that of the NSDAP, was uncomfortable with intellectuals and ideas. The men who controlled the PNF and NSDAP and their youth organizations during the 1930s – Achille Starace, Carlo Scorza, Renato Ricci and Baldur von Schirach – preferred training in physical and military education and lessons in discipline to substantive discussions about ideas. The message was reduced to a celebration of the cult of the Duce, nationalism and militarism. This was thin stuff and boredom accounts for much of the fall in membership numbers in the older age groups. Compounding the problem in Italy was the existence of Catholic religious instruction within the youth organizations carried out by officially designated chaplains. The Church was so pleased by the system that in August 1943, just after the fall of Mussolini, the bishop in charge of religious instruction in the Opera Nazionale Balilia urged the government to continue the organization under Church control.

In Germany, powerful nationalist youth organizations had existed since the nineteenth century. Although the Nazis' main organization, Hitler Jugend (Hitler Youth), had at the moment of the seizure of power a relatively small percentage of the student population, it rapidly coordinated the existing conservative and Protestant organizations. Membership jumped from 107,956 in 1932 to almost 2.3 million at the end of 1933 and to 7 million out of 9 million 10 to 18 year olds in 1938.

As in Fascist Italy, separate organizations for boys and girls existed according to age beginning at age 10 for boys with German Young People, at age 14 with Hitler Jugend (Hitler Youth) and for girls with the Jungmädel (Young Girls) for ages from 10 to 14 and at 14 years the Bund Deutscher Mädel (League of German Girls). Members were required to dress in uniforms, march and drill in paramilitary fashion. As in Italy, the stress was on military and physical education with a mixture of competitions and games. Ideologically, the cult of the Führer, nationalism and military culture, comradeship and racial values were central. Nazi youth education resembled its Fascist counterpart in its ritualized behaviour and lack of respect for ideas that in the long run engendered a degree of boredom. There is no doubt however that the success of Hitler Youth in eliminating competitors, especially those of the Catholic Church, contributed to a greater measure of success in militancy and ideological commitment.

Another advantage that the Nazi regime had in penetrating the schools at all levels was a broad base of initial support among teachers, who had been over-represented in the party from the beginning. By 1934 the NSDAP had 84,000 teacher members or one-quarter of the total in the profession. Eventually, almost all elementary and secondary school teachers belonged to the Nazi Teachers' Association.[12]

The Nazis also conducted a much deeper purge in higher education than did the Fascists. The extent of the purge is surprising because the prevailing university culture was already conservative and nationalist before the Nazi seizure of power. When the Fascists insisted on a loyalty oath in 1931 for university professors, only eleven prominent anti-fascists resigned from their teaching positions. (It should be noted that the regime did not resort to more violent and direct means to conduct the purge.) The Nazi arsenal in the battle against culture contained many more weapons, including the racial standard. The Nazis also went much further by introducing a greater degree of ideological content into higher education. Racial theory, genetics, revised biology and a purged literature with a stress on folklore gained central positions in the curricula leading to the universities. Between 1932 and 1934, the new regime eliminated 1,145 of 7,758 university professors, one third for racial reasons. Noakes and Pridham note that the universities of Berlin and Frankfurt had 32 per cent of their staff dismissed.[13]

Both Nazis and Fascists sought to redirect the school population away from the universities and towards technical training. The Fascist regime, especially, wanted to modernize the schools and make them more responsive to the employment market. To this end, entry to the university was discouraged and students were urged to shift to technical training programmes. The Fascist School Charter of 1939 set up professional and technical secondary schools and considerably lengthened the years of common schooling. In each case, populist anti-intellectualism vied with a conservative vision of social hierarchy and stability to contain the pressure for upward mobility through higher education. The Nazis in 1937 and the Fascist School Charter of 1939 introduced a labour requirement for all students as a further rhetorical bow to the idea of an egalitarian national or racial community. The idea that students be made to do physical labour formed part of the campaign against the individualistic bourgeois lifestyle that so dominated fascist propaganda in the 1930s. But the School Charter did not alter the structure of elite secondary schools that led to the university and did nothing to end the monopoly of classical education. The war broke out before any of its more experimental elements could be tested.

The inability of the Fascists to break the hold of conservative culture over the universities led them to sponsor special national university competitions, open only to members of the GUF. The *littoriali* of art and culture were annual events, held in different cities throughout the peninsula, but by the late 1930s the *littoriali* events took on an air of *fronde* as the young Fascists engaged in their own generation warfare against an ageing Fascist political class.

11 Culture and society

Religion and the Churches

Nowhere are the differences in the contexts within which the Fascist and Nazi regimes operated more revealing than in the general area of religious policy. Mussolini in 1929 and Hitler in 1933 signed concordats with the Vatican to regulate relations between Church and state in their respective countries. They then worked to bend the framework set by the concordats to their own ends. Both regimes offered a quasi-religious vision of a new society and a new type of humanity that would repudiate any religious message of solidarity across national or ethnic lines. Fascism and nazism incorporated religious ritual and symbolism in highly elaborate ceremonies. Nazi party congresses took on aspects of a religious celebration with the cult of the Führer as the centrepiece. Each regime battled with the churches for control of the calendar of holy days. For instance, the Fascist state recognized thirteen Catholic holy days, but flanked them with national or party festivals. The celebrations of the March on Rome (28 October) and the victory over Austria (4 November) coexisted with All Saints' Day (1 November). The anniversary of the founding of the first *fascio* (23 March) and that of the founding of Rome (21 April) conflicted with the celebrations of Easter.[1] Michael Burleigh noted how the Nazis also integrated existing Christian holidays and infused them with new meaning:

> The year commenced with the Day of the Seizure of Power (30 January) and progressed through the Promulgation of the party programme (24 February), Heroes Memorial Day (16 March), the Führer's birthday (20 April), the National Festival of the

German People (1 May), Mothers' Day (May), the Summer
Solstice (21 June), the Reich Party Day (early September),
Harvest Thanksgiving (early October), Commemoration of the
Movement's Fallen (9 November) which replaced Remem-
brance Sunday, and the Winter Solstice (21 December and
Christmas).

Describing the Nazi Commemoration of the Movement's Fallen,
Burleigh concluded: 'This must have been a tear-jerker, prompting
nausea in any fastidious rationalist or person of genuine religious
faith.'[2]

The relative power of the Catholic Church made the situation in
Italy quite different from that in Nazi Germany. Italian Fascists of
all varieties agreed on a few core beliefs: the cult of the Duce, a
strong state and an aggressive foreign policy, but when it came to
religious policy opinion varied widely. Although no serious Fascist
leaders (apart from the demented philosopher Julius Evola) opted
for neopagan ideologies or Nordic cults, at least two parts of the
Fascist coalition were potentially hostile to religion. Influenced by
eighteenth-century rationalism, socialist materialism and resentment
against papal rule in central Italy, Mussolini's upbringing was
steeped in visceral hostility to the Catholic Church. A second, quite
different, position developed out of the neo-Hegelian political philosophy of Giovanni Gentile. Gentile's all-encompassing ethical
state replaced religion as the source of values and served as the basis
for a nationalism that obliterated the distinction between the public
and private spheres by identifying the individual with the national
collectivity.[3] The Catholic Church understood that this philosophical vision expressed fascism's true totalitarian aspiration and kept
much of Gentile's philosophical output on the Index of Forbidden
Books. Potentially anti-Catholic traditions were countered by
others who were not hostile to Catholicism. Most Italian national-
ists, while not always personally religious, viewed the Catholic
Church as a monument to Italian genius, and a large number of
Fascist conservatives were simply practising Catholics.

The Fascists lacked the Nazis' overriding belief in the power of
race as the determining force in history. This sweeping, profoundly
subversive theory that denied any universal standards of morality
across racial lines was fundamentally at odds with traditional religion. None of the major Nazi leaders belonged to traditional

Christian churches; many, including Hitler, were atheists; others, like Hess and Rosenberg, adhered to variants of Nordic pagan cults.

Ideological differences apart, the Fascist regime faced a national church that influenced everything from high culture to popular customs and morality. The Catholic Church in Italy emerged from its nineteenth-century battle with the liberal state in control of a strong network of financial, social and educational institutions. After 1900, the Church and Italy's conservative elites allied against the Socialist movement. Although the Roman question was still unsettled, the First World War brought the Italian Church even closer to the national cause.

In Germany the Catholic Church was a regional force that faced a hostile state after 1870. The Catholic Centre party had been forged in the struggle against Bismarck's Kulturkampf, but the need for a formal political party was a sign of political weakness and insecurity more than of strength. By necessity, the Church sought defensive concessions that might allow it to secure its regional base. In contrast, the Italian hierarchy represented a force that had always believed itself to be co-equal to the state.

At first, Hitler and Mussolini faced the problem of winning the benevolent neutrality of the Catholic hierarchy in order to undermine the Popular and Centre parties. For the Church, no friend of parliamentary democracy, the task was to win sufficient concessions in direct negotiations with the government. In Italy, where a stable alliance between Church and state developed, the initial steps were slow. When Mussolini was feeling his way from October 1922 until the Matteotti murder, the Fascist government bailed out the Catholic-controlled Banco di Roma, introduced Catholic catechism in the elementary schools and allowed the crucifix in classrooms and public buildings in a successful campaign to entice the Church to abandon the Popular (Catholic) party, which had opposed the Fascist electoral reform.

Relations were put on hold during the crisis over Matteotti in 1924 and 1925, but, even then, the Vatican rendered a singular service to the government when it forbade the surviving Catholic political forces to join any common front with socialists. After 1925 negotiations slowly and painstakingly led to the Lateran Treaty and Concordat of 11 February 1929.

The Fascist regime obtained four major advantages from the Lateran treaty. First, it was able to incorporate the Catholic Church within the consensus behind the new state. Second, the Fascist government gained the support of the Church in its efforts to reach the Catholic rural masses. Third, the government increased its international prestige, especially among foreign Catholics. Finally, the Fascists won from the Church a promise to dissolve its political youth organizations.

In return, the Vatican state was created with full sovereign rights. The state recognized the central role of Catholic doctrine in the elementary and middle-school curriculum and on basic questions of public morality, such as divorce. Realizing that this was an enormous concession for a regime that professed its own 'total' vision, Gentile spoke against the agreements during the Italian Senate debates. The Church also won an autonomous sphere within which it could develop those institutions not deemed political, such as the Catholic University of Milan, Catholic university groups, the Catholic Action, diocesan social groups and various publishing initiatives.

The influx of Catholic support after 1929 created a clerical fascism, which vied with other ideologies for the 'true fascist' mantle. During the 1930s the power and prestige of the Church increased as the ideological vacuum of fascism became more apparent. Indeed, at this time the Church managed to train almost the entire postwar Christian Democratic political class, as well as convert a number of powerful Fascist leaders. The Church succeeded because the regime did not challenge Italian Catholics with fundamental moral dilemmas. In contrast, deeply religious Germans retreated from the public sphere rather than apply policies of sterilization, abortion, euthanasia and generalized racial persecution. Even when confronted by the Italian racial legislation of 1938, the Church was willing to tolerate a certain degree of religious (as against racial) discrimination against the Jews. Thus, rather than retreating into a private sphere, Catholics were able to fill a vacuum in the public arena with their own version of fascism.

The concordat between the Nazi regime and the Vatican of 8 July 1933 followed the broad lines of the earlier agreement with Mussolini. Central to both was the abandonment by the Church of its overtly political apparatus, but the survival of its social and religious organizations. The Nazi regime, again like its Fascist counterpart, won both domestic and international prestige. The Catholic Church supported many of the foreign policy initiatives of both regimes, such as the Ethiopian War, Italian intervention in the Spanish Civil War, the reannexation of the Saar in 1935 and the incorporation of Austria into the Reich in 1938. However, the weaker German Church gained much less from the German concordat. The Nazi regime formally recognized the regional strength of the Church: the continued existence of Catholic schools, religious freedom, and the survival of a network of diocesan organizations.

In both countries Catholic youth organizations became the flashpoint of conflict, in 1931 the Vatican publicly protested about measures taken against Catholic Action's youth organizations and a compromise was worked out under which the Catholics gave up their uniforms and distinctive symbols. The German regime allowed the Church an even more limited autonomy. Dual membership in Nazi and Catholic organizations was banned. Police surveillance and censorship limited the impact of any gestures of opposition that did take place and finally Catholic youth movements were dissolved in 1937.

The Nazi relationship with the Protestant Evangelical Church had no counterpart in Fascist Italy. Nonetheless, it reveals something of the way fascist-style regimes dealt with bedrock institutions. At first, the Nazis thought to take over the Evangelical Church by unifying it under the leadership of the German Christian movement. The German Christians accepted the notion of a racial community that coincided with the church community. In church elections in mid-1933 they won roughly two-thirds of the posts and pro-Nazi Bishop Ludwig Müller was catapulted into a position of leadership. References to the Judaic origins of Christianity, not to mention actual Jewish converts to the Evangelical faith, were to be banished from the race-based religious community.

The radical re-working of religious doctrine and the crude tactics of the Nazi sympathizers provoked a reaction. In September 1933, a Pastors' Emergency League was set up under the leadership of Martin Niemöller; then in April 1934, the Confessional Church was organized to oppose the German Christian leadership. The Confessional Church produced the Barmen Confession of May 1934, which restated traditional values. At that point, Hitler decided to step back from the warring factions and abandoned Bishop Müller to his fate. The result, however, was far from a victory for any anti-Nazi resistance. The leadership of the Confessing Church with few exceptions accommodated itself to Nazi rule over the state and was content to remain within its increasingly narrow sphere of influence.

Religious resistance to Hitler on the part of both Catholics and Protestants was limited to those instances when the Nazi regime over-stepped certain boundaries. It was most often a battle waged on the local level with ordinary church-goers defending their right to have crucifixes in classrooms or to march in religious processions. A Nazi decree that All Saints' Day and the Feast of the Epiphany would no longer be public holidays provoked resistance in strongly Catholic areas. Occasionally, the hierarchy took a stand. The Archbishop of Münster, Clemens von Galen, condemned the Nazi euthanasia programme in a sermon on 3 August 1941, but the earlier sterilization program could not have been effective without the participation of many religious educational and medical institutions. The faithful in Italy and Germany generally supported the policies of their governments, especially when they reflected shared values, such as the struggle against communism.

Culture

Although profound differences existed between the Italian and German varieties of fascism over cultural policies, the two regimes shared some mechanisms of control and certain biases in art and architecture. Fascism and Nazism specifically rejected internationalism, however differently interpreted in art and culture. Both regimes reasserted a 'national' tradition, expressed as a broadly conceived realism and a return to classical models and solidity of form.[4] Both used a corporative framework for state intervention in the organization of culture, but neither fully centralized control of cultural policy in a single place. The same overlapping jurisdictions and infighting that existed in other areas plagued efforts to set a cultural agenda. Finally, the Fascist and Nazi regimes won a great deal of passive support from cultural producers through a range of specific benefits that were offered to artists, architects, musicians and theatre professionals within the corporative framework. These ranged from competitions and commissions to better copyright protection, regulation of standards for entry into professions and increased public monies for theatre and film.[5]

Recent research on the cultural policies of Italian fascism has put to rest the idea that the creative arts and cultural pluralism were dead under the dictatorship. In fact, the continuities between the pre-First World War culture and Fascist culture during the 1920s and between the youth culture of the 1930s and post-1943 neo-realism have emerged ever more strongly. Unlike the Nazis, who applied a rigorous racial standard to intellectual life and clear stylistic preferences in the arts, the Fascists had no ready-made criteria with which to judge the creative arts. Their pluralism was connected to the 'fascist style of rule' that developed on the peninsula. Mussolini's dictatorship not only Balkanized the state, but it also left traditional power centres with control over their own cultural agendas. Most cultural trends found patrons in this fragmented system, but at the cost of working within the framework set by the state and for the overall objectives of the regime. Intellectuals were often given freedom to debate cultural issues only as long as the regime felt they served a purpose. Just as suddenly, orders would go out to cease and the issues would disappear from the newspapers and journals.[6]

During the 1920s four initiatives emerged. Two of these, the National Fascist Institute of Culture and the project for the *Italian Encyclopedia*, were under the control of the philosopher Giovanni Gentile. Gentile, as Minister of Public Instruction from 1922 to 1924, had resisted efforts to purge the universities and held to his view that higher culture could not be coerced, but only absorbed into a developing national consciousness. For the *Italian Encyclopedia* project, his strategy of seeking the best experts in each field without regard to political affiliation co-opted neutral and anti-fascist intellectuals into a major undertaking of the regime at the price of diluting its fascist character.

A third institution, the Italian Royal Academy, announced in 1926, and launched in 1929, became a bastion of conservative and establishment culture during the remaining years of the regime. It represented a wider phenomenon that had a parallel in Nazi Germany of bringing all cultural and scientific organizations under the control of the Fascist state. This process went in two directions. The regime began to centralize in Rome what had been a diffused and provincial cultural landscape. It also absorbed pre-Fascist cultural and scientific institutions. These ranged from the Agrarian Society of Bologna to the Petrarch Academy of Arezzo. Loyalty oaths were used to drive prominent opponents out. In 1931 an oath was imposed on university teachers and in 1933 the same oath was extended to all members of cultural and scientific academies. The final step came in 1939 with the incorporation of Italy's most prestigious and venerable academy, the *Lincei*, into the *Accademia d'Italia*.[7]

But both regimes went further. In both Fascist Italy and Nazi Germany, the state began to draw into its orbit large areas of professional life. Both regimes rejected the notion of the pure or uncommitted intellectual or the apolitical professional. In both regimes the state offered concrete economic advantages to the professions in exchange for integrating into the framework of the regime. In the context of high unemployment and overcrowding in many of the professions, the regime's corporative structures provided both a bureaucratic refuge and a source of patronage. Professionals, such as engineers and architects, had pressed even before the coming of fascism for official recognition of their status and a system of state registration and responded favourably to the overtures of the regimes.

In Italy the process began with the April 1926 Rocco law, which established on officially recognized syndical organization for each economic and professional category. In 1928, the Confederation of Professional and Artists Syndicates was established; in 1934, it was transformed into the Corporation of Artists and Professionals. These official syndical organizations maintained registers of members. Journalists were among the first to be registered and controlled in 1925. In 1926 an oath was imposed on lawyers and all legal officers to carry out duties in the higher interests of the nation. Regulation of the legal profession was designed both assure political conformity and to control access to a crowded profession. The next year teachers were forced to pledge that they would not belong to parties or associations that the state deemed incompatible with their position. Loyalty oaths were extended in 1931 to university faculties and to all scientific and cultural academies. But even earlier in 1928, university instructors had been required to give up membership in associations or parties that were incompatible with their position and individuals could be excluded from state competitions for political reasons. Finally, in 1938, a law was passed that established a state interest in all professional activity and made obligatory enrollment on the registers of professional organizations. When the racial laws of 1938 were decreed, these registers became part of the process for excluding Jews.[8] By 1940 the percentage of membership in official organizations was extremely high: 85 per cent of journalists and notaries, 77 per cent of doctors, 70 per cent of architects, 81 per cent of pharmacists, 66 per cent of engineers.[9] For creative artists membership in the official organizations became a *sine qua non* to compete in the important exhibitions, such as the Venice Biennale, the Triennale of Milan, and the Quadriennale d'Arte Nazionale in Rome and for the lucrative commissions that were controlled by the regime, although it should be noted that no single school dominated these competitions and exhibits.

The 1930s saw additional power centres superimposed. The Fascists had always exercised strict controls over the daily press, but the 1930s saw a tightening of the screw. Impressed by Goebbels' new Ministry of Propaganda, Mussolini's son-in-law, Galeazzo Ciano, expanded the press office, which he headed in 1933, to become a Secretariat for Press and Propaganda with supervision of the film industry. The Secretariat was transformed into a ministry in 1935 and then became the Ministry of Popular Culture (Minculpop) under Alessandro Pavolini in 1937. Centralized control was extended over film, newspapers and the radio. However, the Minculpop failed to establish fixed criteria for the censorship of literary and scholarly works. Throughout the 1920s and early 1930s works by Bolshevik economists, major Soviet and American authors and leading writers of the European avant-garde circulated widely.[10]

All films, domestic or foreign, were subjected to censorship but relatively few were pieces of overt propaganda. Both regimes allowed, even encouraged, a large measure of popular diversion, although each made propaganda films and stressed documentary newsreels. American film products had a larger share of the Italian market and the most popular films in both Italy and Germany were escapist comedies. In Italy at least, the result was to encourage a quite ambiguous myth of America and of its consumer society. Fascist intellectuals were often disapproving, but the popular reaction was certainly very different.[11]

The differences that existed between Italy and Germany were not so much in intent as in the technical apparatus available to each regime. For instance, Germany had a much larger film industry and a far more extensive radio network than the Italians. The impact of Italian state-controlled radio was limited by the poverty of the country and the cost of receivers. More than half of the schools did not have radios by 1938 and a year later Italy had only 1.2 million radio subscriptions as against Germany's 12 million.

As usual, control over culture was subject to the same fragmentation of power that we have found in other areas of Fascist administration. The impact of the Ministry of Popular Culture was limited by rival power centres. One existed after 1937 in the Ministry of National Education where long-time cultural entrepreneur Giuseppe Bottai deliberately pursued an eclectic arts policy. Outside of government, the Catholic Church developed its own cultural network.[12] The old liberal culture survived under the protection of Benedetto Croce, Italy's most illustrious philosopher, and around the liberal economist Luigi Einaudi and his son Giulio. Finally, the Fascist hard-liner, Roberto Farinacci, used his provincial power base to foster the style of art favoured by the Nazis.

These competing voices meant that Fascists remained deeply divided over fundamental issues such as modernity versus tradition, the relationship of Italian to European and American culture and the position of the Catholic Church in Italian society. All agreed that post-Risorgimental liberal Italy was found wanting but there was no consensus on the conclusions that might be drawn from this. Mussolini himself embodied many of these contradictions. Early in his career he had been associated with a modernizing counterculture. F. T. Marinetti's Futurist movement rallied to the original *Fascio di Combattimento*. This Fascism of 1919 was a product of the war and of Milan, Italy's most advanced city. Even later, the Duce never completely lost his fascination for the modern. His original inspiration continued to exist even when submerged in the traditionalist bourgeois culture of acceptable fascism after 1921. He wanted fascism to be identified with dynamism, speed, action and combat, although he never fulfilled Marinetti's hopes to see futurism recognized as the official art of the regime.

Both the Fascist and Nazi regimes manipulated modern technology in the pursuit of a distinctive cultural style. Josef Goebbels understood the importance of film, radio, striking visuals and the manipulation of subliminal messages. If anything, the Fascists were even more creative in their borrowing because they were less inhibited about accepting forms of contemporary art and architecture. The 1932 Mostra della Rivoluzione Fascista was a triumph in the way it conveyed a message through modern graphics and architecture, but the Fascists borrowed from every modernist school including Soviet constructivism and the Bauhaus to create their exhibition to commemorate the coming to power of the Duce.[13]

The 1930s brought this somewhat chaotic system to a point of crisis. Relations with the western liberal democracies deteriorated after 1935 and cultural reactionaries were able to accentuate their campaigns against the decadent, pluto-democratic systems of America, England and France. The current of cultural pessimism that underlay both fascism and nazism came to the fore in warnings about a loss of spirituality, rootedness and humanism in the face of cosmopolitanism and internationalism. Efforts were made to impose a kind of spiritual autarky on Italy after the outbreak of the Ethiopian war. Although the move failed, it received an ominous boost from the official anti-Semitism and racism after 1938.[14]

The disintegration of the cultural consensus around the nationalist core of Fascist ideology became apparent in the regime's inability to deal with the new generation that it had educated and which came of age in the 1930s. For a decade the Fascists had denounced the old liberal individualistic culture as moribund and inadequate for a modern mass society. Fascism proclaimed itself as the only alternative to a dying capitalism and an alien Bolshevism. Young intellectuals took seriously the call for social revolution, creation of a mass culture and corporative institutions. This disquiet was translated into a movement for literary and cinematographic realism, but it soon became apparent that strict limits would be imposed on experimentation in a regime of autarky and war mobilization.[15]

Nazi Germany presented some similarities and several sharp contrasts to the situation in Fascist Italy. Both regimes integrated cultural and scientific societies into the framework of the state and both sought to control the 'free' professions. In Germany the depression had created extraordinarily high levels of unemployment and increased the intensity of competition in professions such as law, medicine, and engineering. Konrad Jarausch stressed the generational aspect of the problem: 'By the year 1931, 550,000 young unemployed and 40,000 superfluous academics seemed to block all prospects for the future.'[16] The Nazis moved in two directions to resolve this problem. They drastically reduced access to higher education, which became less and less open to the lower middle class. University attendance dropped from 60,148 to 41,069 between 1936 and 1938 but it was less than two-fifths of the 1931 peak year. Law school registrations dropped from 8026 to 4275, in the philosophy faculty from 17,760 to 12,240, and in the engineering schools from 11,794 to 9347. The Nazis also took over or established new organizations for lawyers, teachers, engineers and other professional groups immediately after the seizure of power. As in Italy, many of the organizations were easily persuaded to cooperate, willingly accepted pro-Nazi leadership, and took the required oaths of loyalty in exchange for professional recognition and some form of employment security.[17]

The major difference between the two regimes came with the use of racial criteria that put in the hands of the National Socialists a weapon that they used to purge culture to an extent unimaginable on the peninsula. It took the Fascists over a decade to create a propaganda ministry; the Nazis accomplished the feat in little more than a month after taking power. Josef Goebbels was named to head the new Reich Ministry for Public Enlightenment and Propaganda on 13 March 1933. Goebbels's ministry seemed to have ensured its cultural monopoly through the Reich Culture Chamber, created on 22 September 1933 with subdivisions for the various branches: press, music, theatre, visual arts, literature. After 1 November 1933, to work as a professional in any of these fields required a permit from the responsible chamber and it was virtually impossible to survive without it. Coupled with the racial laws and the campaign against cultural Bolshevism, the Nazi regime had powerful weapons to control the gamut of culture and to offer the options of exile or adherence to the goals of the state.

The April 1933 Law for the Restoration of the Civil Service, which had such a limited impact on the bureaucracy in general, was devastating for culture. For instance, the government dismissed twenty museum directors as part of the purge of the arts establishment. All modern art was deemed Judeo-Bolshevik and was subject to removal without regard to particular schools or even to the racial category of the artist. In fact, only six of the 112 artists included in the Nazi Degenerate Art Exhibition of 1937 were Jews.[18]

In place of art deemed degenerate, the Nazis drew on Greco Roman classical models, German medieval and ruralist genre painting. To ensure against any possibility of dissent, in November 1936

Goebbels banned all art criticism (something that would have been inconceivable in Italy) and restricted critics to mere descriptive reviews.[19] But the National Socialists went further by encouraging the physical destruction of the works they opposed. In May 1933, public burning of books took place in many university centres, although the books in question were often still available until after 1935 when a confidential index of banned books was drawn up. Museums faced even more drastic constraints: hundreds of works of art were destroyed and many more were sold at auction to end up in museums and private collections outside of Germany. Architecture was especially hard hit. The Bauhaus was shut down and public commissions no longer went to architects working in the international style, although many less visible and utilitarian buildings continued to be designed along rationalist lines. Official architecture in the Third Reich tended towards the classical monumental, but without the interesting fusion of rationalist elements with the monumental that took place in Italy.

Nonetheless, Nazi cultural policy was marked by the same jurisdictional conflicts that developed in Fascist Italy but, in contrast to the Italian case, the conflicts of overlapping jurisdictions seemed to create conditions for further rigidity rather than for increased pluralism. Initially, Goebbels moved cautiously and sought compromise with the conservative establishment. He appointed Richard Strauss to head the Music Chamber and initially worked well with him on copyright legislation and other immediate benefits. But the strategy backfired when Strauss refused to break off his collaboration with the Jewish writer Stefan Zweig.[20] Goebbels also showed some toleration for expressionist art, but found himself forced to accommodate the party's chief ideologue, Alfred Rosenberg, who headed the Fighting League for German Culture and had distinct views on art. Rosenberg challenged Goebbels's relaxed attitude towards artists like Emil Nolde and ultimately won Hitler's support for a general denunciation of an expressionist primitivism that seemed to draw its inspiration from too many non-western sources.[21] Nor were Wilhelm Frick's Interior Ministry, Bernhard Rust's Education Ministry, the Nazi Press Bureau of Otto Dietrich and the Censorship Office under Philipp Bouhler out of the picture. Individual Nazis, notably Hermann Göring, assumed a role as patron of the arts.[22]

Any comparison of the number of exiles from Italy and Germany confirms the vast differences between Fascist and Nazi cultural policies. Few intellectuals and artists left Italy for exile compared to the roster of the leading names of German intellectual life to flee nazism, and several of the most notable Italians, such as Arturo Toscanini and Enrico Fermi, departed only in the late 1930s when the climate became more repressive.

Yet the differences should not be attributed to any inherent tolerance on the part of Italians or repressive tendencies of the Germans. Liberal intellectuals such as Piero Gobetti and Giovanni Amendola were murdered by Fascist thugs in the 1920s. The Fascist political police with the aid of the French right-wing terrorist organization, the Cagoule, reached into France to assassinate Carlo and Nello Rosselli in 1937. Communist and democratic agents, infiltrated back into the country, usually lasted no more than a few months before they were caught by the extremely effective network of informers and spies. More than any supposed Italian humanity versus German barbarism that saved fascism from the worst excesses, it was the structural compromises made during the 1920s that conditioned Italian fascism throughout the 1930s and kept the regime from following the German model. How long these compromises might have held in a Nazi-dominated Europe is a matter of conjecture.

12 Consensus and coercion under fascism and nazism

Any measurement of consensus in a regime built on repression of dissent and on political violence as an acceptable means of resolving disputes is problematic at best. Josef Goebbels's reputation as a master of the art of propaganda has given the impression that the Germans had been reduced to passive recipients of material produced by the regime. But we have now come to understand that the situation was more complex. The gap between the purported Fascist and Nazi revolutions and what actually took place in the towns and countryside was great.[1] Neither regime had sufficient time to overcome the resistance of long-established institutions to their totalizing ambitions. Fascist and Nazi populism and the ideal of a national or racial community were intended to bridge the gap and, over the long term, to create a new social reality, but that order had not been achieved by the outbreak of the Second World War, although it went further in Nazi Germany than in Fascist Italy.

Consensus under both the Fascists and the Nazis was created in part by the physical elimination of alternatives and by the intimidation of opponents. In both regimes a separate system of justice and policing was set up for political crimes. Liberty could be limited by official decree without recourse to regular courts. However, significant differences existed between the two regimes. The Fascists kept the repressive apparatus in the hands of the regular police bureaucracy. The OVRA, the Italian secret police, was headed by bureaucrats from the Interior ministry like Arturo Bocchini and Carmine Senise. In contrast, Party men like Heinrich Himmler and Reinhard Heydrich, moved from control of the SS organization to total centralized control of the state police in 1936.

The mass of Italians and Germans who voted Socialist or Communist did not become Fascists and Nazis; many were reduced to silence after their political and trade union organizations were smashed and their neighbourhoods terrorized by black- and brown-shirted thugs. In our rush to analyse fascist propaganda and political religion, it is easy to forget that the regimes were built on fear and force. Even after the Fascist regime consolidated its power, it continued to spy on and intimidate actual and potential opponents. During the years from 1931 to 1938, the national police (Carabinieri), 50,000 strong, made 579,341 arrests, based on over 33 million police reports, 13,105 condemnations to forced domicile, and 31,493 police warnings.[2] By the late 1930s police controls extended beyond political opponents to any signs of deviation in the general population. Extensive files were kept, regular censorship of mail was carried out; political opponents were subjected to physical and psychological violence. In addition to Jews after 1938, Jehovah's Witnesses and other Protestant denominations were subjected to increased surveillance as the regime sought to homogenize ever more the population. With the coming of the war, the Fascist regime began to establish perhaps fifty concentration camps for interned foreign Jews, prisoners of war from Greece and Yugoslavia, and certain Italian political prisoners. The largest were at Ferramonti di Tarsia in the province of Cosenza and at Renicci, near Arezzo. While not comparable to the Nazi large-scale camp system, they were indications that the regime was moving to control the population by separating out undesirables.[3]

Numbers in Nazi concentration camps varied widely before the war. Immediately after the seizure of power in 1933 perhaps 100,000 political oppnenents were held in SA camps that were often unofficial and subject to no rules. As the regime consolidated its power, prisoners were released so that by the mid-1930s the camps, now official and under SS control, held only several thousand, but with the radicalization after 1938 the camps expanded rapidly both in number of camps and prisoners held.

However, we also know that the regimes could not have survived on pure violence. For one, the police forces at their disposition were not large enough. Robert Gellately's study of the Nazi police showed that the number of Gestapo agents was relatively small. For instance in Düsseldorf with a population of a half million there were only 126 officials, Essen had 43 agents for a population of 650,000. Numbers for the OVRA were similar. Effectiveness in both cases was built on a network of block and neighbourhood informants who willingly denounced their neighbours and associates for passing remarks, listening to foreign radio broadcasts, and in Germany, violations of the racial laws.[4] This network also indirectly made the political police in both regimes a major source of information on the state of public opinion.

'Consensus' undeniably rested on some positive elements. The cult of the Duce or Führer was central to both regimes. The propaganda machines were extremely effective in establishing the direct relationship between leader and masses. Both Hitler and Mussolini was very conscious of how their images were presented to the people. No doubt German enthusiasm for Hitler was genuine and the Italian archives are full of direct appeals to the Duce from workers and peasants for favours.[5]

As might be expected, intellectuals led the fawning crowd. Before the First World War, calls for a strong man to step forward to reverse the process of degeneration were common in anti-democratic literature. During the Fascist and Nazi regimes the essential role of the great leader became a dogma. Josef Goebbels ascribed religious qualities to Hitler. The intelligent and sensitive Giuseppe Bottai called his the generation of Mussolini and linked his own destiny to that of the Duce.

However, consensus must be measured differently for the leaders and for their movements. There is no doubt that Mussolini and Hitler were more popular than either the PNF or NSDAP, and to some extent built their popularity at the expense of the movements. Hitler was not above exploiting the purge of the unruly SA to enhance his image as guarantor of order. Mussolini's refusal to appoint a popular secretary of the PNF indicated an unwillingness to see the party become the base of a political challenge.[6]

To this extent, the popularity of the leaders was a measure of their ability to reassure the population that they would act as guarantors of stability. For instance, both leaders stressed the struggle against Bolshevism and revolutionary social upheaval. In the case of Hitler this is quite significant. Anti-Semitism did not appeal to the German people throughout the period from 1929 to 1939 as much as did economic and social issues. During their rise to power, the Nazis stressed anti-socialist themes and the struggle for employment. They projected the vision of the *Volksgemeinschaft* in which merit and effort would be rewarded.

Peace, stability and order enhanced the consensus. Most Germans and Italians had no idea of the basic instability of regimes built on the unbridled ambitions of a handful of individuals. For Mussolini, the image of trains running on time and a society at work, on reclamation projects and the building of new cities captured the popular imagination, as did Hitler's claim that he put Germany back to work. Both leaders understood and cultivated this image. As their societies moved towards military mobilization during the late 1930s, the Duce and the Führer opted for guns *and* butter. Both regimes tended to relax in practice the anti-labour policies of the early years. Hitler never forgot the breakdown of German morale at the end of the First World War and Mussolini remembered the strikes to protest the cost of living in Turin in 1917. The German regime ensured that basic food supplies would be adequate during the expected short wars contemplated by Hitler. Mussolini allowed the Fascist unions to reactivate their factory representatives and to press for higher wages in 1937 and 1938.

A second theme in both regimes was foreign policy. Neither leader portrayed himself as a war leader. Rather, both stressed diplomatic successes at a limited risk. They played on wounded national feelings by showing that their nations were now respected. The Duce was able to build popularity during the depression without exploiting the foreign policy card, but his move into Ethiopia and successful defiance of League of Nations sanctions brought his acclaim to the highest point in early 1936. The German alliance that followed was never popular, and Mussolini's prestige received a devastating blow in March 1938 when Hitler marched into Austria. It recovered in September of that year when the Duce seemed to engineer the peaceful settlement of the Czech dispute at Munich. Similarly, Hitler's popularity peaked with the easy victories over the remilitarization of the Rhineland in March 1936 and the *Anschluss* with Austria two years later. The Munich crisis increased doubts that were only temporarily alleviated in 1939. Hitler's rapid victories in 1940 again brought renewed popularity in the hope that peace could be restored. Subsequently, both the Führer and his regime steadily declined in favour after 1942.[7]

The methods used in the Fascist and Nazi regimes to achieve consensus went beyond the propagation of the myth of the Duce or Führer. As has already been noted, the search for a binding set of myths that might hold mass society together was a staple in antidemocratic circles of both right and left since the end of the nineteenth century. Sorel, Barrès, Pareto, Le Bon, Moeller van den Bruck, Spengler, Corradini, Papini and the young Mussolini in one way or another all touched on problems of politics under conditions of universal suffrage and mass mobilization. Fascism in Italy and Germany was a deliberately conceived response to this challenge. Despite differences in message, the intent was exactly the same: to provide a quasi-religious alternative to Marxism. Central to this was the idea of a national rebirth in a new social and political system, which would overcome the dichotomies, inherent in modern industrial capitalism, between private and public, individual and collective. Such aspirations certainly had the totalizing qualities found in many mass religious movements. In Fascist Italy a conscious effort was made to infuse the regime with quasi-religious ritual and symbolism.[8] The new Fascist calendar not only harked back to the French Revolution, but also to the origins of Christianity. The passage from the youth organizations to the PNF, the *leva fascista,* clearly mirrored Catholic confirmation. Similarly, ceremonies for martyrs to the cause, the profusion of banners and rituals, even the establishment of a *Scuola della Mistica fascista* attested to the religious vocation of the movement, as did the highly choreographed mass rallies, the banners, the cult of the fallen and the elements of Aryan worship in the Nazi movement.

The vexing determination to alter public behaviour by the imposition of the Hitler salute or the abolition of the supposedly foreign and feminine *lei* and its substitution with *voi* as the formal form of address in Italian can best be understood as efforts to abolish the idea of the citizen and to fuse the individual with the mass. The two dictatorships sought to shape a new type of humanity; but, as their profound distrust of the working class and their acknowledged inability to overcome the bourgeois lifestyle proved, they had far to go before reaching their goal.

In a sense, by the late 1930s, both regimes were violating the compact with parts of the bourgeois coalition that brought them to power. For the Nazis, who commanded a state apparatus that was technically superior, this was not a major obstacle, but for the

Fascists it turned out to be fatal. With the German alliance, the racial campaign and an increasingly risky foreign policy, Mussolini was leading the Italians, including a large part of the political class, in directions they did not wish to go.

13 The status of the military

Initially, the military was granted autonomous status under the Fascists and the Nazis. The neo-feudal model of state organization, adopted by both Mussolini and Hitler, made the military one of the many competing power centres. Traditionally, the military derived its special status from the persistence of the feudal ties to the sovereign that were only partly disrupted by the Weimar Republic and not at all in pre-Fascist Italy. Far more than the Italian generals before the advent of fascism, the German military had become a political elite that played a pivotal role in the life and death of the Weimar Republic.

The relationship of the Italian military to the Fascist movement was probably closer than the German army to its Nazi counterpart before the seizure of power. Most Italian officers sympathized with fascism in 1921 and 1922 and the army provided trucks and weapons to the Fascist squads in their assaults on the Socialist and Communist left in rural Italy. Mussolini directly appealed to the military with promises to improve the material conditions within the officer corps and to restore to the army the place of honour that had been threatened during the revolutionary years of 1919 and 1920. Although the high command assured King Victor Emmanuel that the armed forces would do their duty on 28 October 1922, if martial law were proclaimed to stop the Fascist March on Rome, Marshal Diaz, the commander-in-chief, also made it clear that the army would prefer not to be put to the test and that some sort of compromise be worked out with Mussolini and his followers. It was an important factor in persuading the king to reject the Facta government's request for emergency powers and to open the way to a Fascist government.

Hitler made similar appeals for military support before taking power, most notably at the 1930 trial of three pro-Nazi Reichswehr officers who were accused of treason for preparing the violent over-throw of the constitution. At this trial Hitler testified that the Nazi movement never intended to undermine military discipline or to seize power by any but legal means. Despite these overtures, Hindenburg's personal distaste for Hitler and the efforts of General Kurt von Schleicher, the last chancellor before Hitler, to split the Nazi movement in order to stabilize his own government in late 1932, posed real obstacles to Hitler's assumption of power.

Once Mussolini and Hitler took office, the military reaction was remarkably similar. In 1933, Hindenburg, rather than Hitler, appointed General von Blomberg as War Minister, just as Victor Emmanuel named Marshal Armando Diaz and Admiral Paolo Thaon di Revel to the War and Navy Ministries. But the willingness of the two highest ranking military officers to serve in Mussolini's government was in itself somewhat remarkable. While the king made the appointments to the army and naval ministries, the partic-ipation of Diaz and Thaon di Revel eliminated the traditional dis-tance that had existed between civilian politicians and the military. The monarch affirmed with these appointments the traditional relationship between the ruler and the military establishment; the military ended the practice of appointing civilians to the army ministry; and Mussolini's new government gained credibility.

A parting of the ways between the two regimes in their handling of the military as an institutional force came about a year later when Hindenburg died and Hitler became both Head of Government (Reichskanzler), and Head of State (Führer). From that moment, Hitler could benefit from an exclusive oath of loyalty to his person that Mussolini could never exact as long as the monarchy was still in existence. The Italian military operated with divided loyalties, although they were never tested until 1943 when Marshal Pietro Badoglio was appointed by the king to succeed Mussolini.

The overall context within which the military worked differed considerably in Germany and in Italy. In Italy the conservative fellow travellers gained in power and influence when Mussolini was substantially weakened during the Matteotti crisis. Not only did the military have behind it the monarchy with its special Piedmontese traditions that competed with those of the regime, but it also had powerful economic and social allies and a much less serious rival in the Fascist party. After the murder of Socialist deputy Giacomo Matteotti in 1924, the War Minister General Antonino Di Giorgio backed the beleaguered Duce with an offer to arm the Fascist militias, yet, in 1925, Mussolini was forced to abandon Di Giorgio when the latter's proposed army reform proved unacceptable to the military establishment. As part of a larger political transaction, the Italian officer corps accepted the party card and some propaganda in the barracks, but the Italian high command also succeeded in ridding itself of any competition from a viable Fascist party paramilitary organization. The armed forces maintained considerable autonomy within the regime. Mussolini's personal relationship with the military chiefs was founded on the understanding that the Duce would set overall policy, but that the internal operations of the military, including promotions and preference, would be left to the officer corps. This arrangement, coming as it did on the heels of Di Giorgio's failed military reorganization, thwarted any fundamental reform of the armed forces. As the military historian, Giorgio Rochat, put it:

> The organization of 1926 was the expression of an army that closed in on itself, not only from the political point of view (the nature of the regime that it contributed to create left to the military only space for the defense of their corporate autonomy with much less possibility of influencing the general direction of the country than under the liberal regimes), but also from the technical point of view.[1]

After mid-1933 the German army was forced to manoeuvre without the traditional right-wing political forces and it faced powerful rivals from within the Nazi movement. The German high command viewed with extreme disfavour the extraordinary growth of the SA after 30 January 1933. Röhm's organization, which incorporated some of the most radical and violent parts of the Nazi movement, seemed well on its way to becoming a serious rival to the army. The military was deeply involved in the purge of the SA carried out in June 1934 by the SS even though prominent officers also fell victim to the orgy of vengeance. However, the army's victory over the SA proved short-lived. The German military, once free of SA competition, faced an even more serious challenge from the SS and its armed formations. SS leaders Heinrich Himmler and

Reinhard Heydrich parlayed their control of the Bavarian police in 1933 and of the Prussian police in April 1934 into a unified police command over the entire Reich by 1936, and then won Hitler's consent to form military units in August 1938. The Waffen SS became an additional branch of the military.

The role of the supreme leader and the nature, pace, and timing of military rearmament further distinguished the two regimes. The fact that Mussolini himself held the three military ministries from 1925 to 1929 and again from 1933 to 1943 only compounded the problems that developed in Italy's military preparedness. The Duce did not use his personal authority to force modernization or greater coordination among the three branches and his under-secretaries were reluctant to act on their own. In contrast to Hitler who reordered the system of promotion in the German military but then gave considerable latitude to those whom he appointed, Mussolini's mistrust of his own subordinates and his refusal to allow them to build any independent power base worked against cross-service cooperation. Marshal Pietro Badoglio was appointed commander-in-chief of the army in 1925. Two years later, in 1927, he also became chief of the general staff, but almost immediately lost the command of the army. From 1929 to 1933 he served as governor of Libya and, content to exercise indirect control over the army through client generals, he abandoned any effort whatsoever to coordinate policy among the three services.

From 1922 to 1933, it made little sense for Italy to pour significant sums into the military, and the onset of the Great Depression forced deeper cuts in all government expenditures including the military budget. In contrast to Nazi Germany, the Italian military did not immediately assume a central role in Mussolini's plans. Limited budgets meant that military strategy concentrated on holding the line against France, on operations in defence of Austria, and on possible offensive action against Yugoslavia. Good relations with Britain were taken for granted, and, in the case of Badoglio, France was viewed with some sympathy, while Germany remained suspect.

Beginning with the war in Ethiopia in late 1935 and Italy's intervention in the Spanish Civil War in July 1936, the regime abruptly reversed direction and increased military expenditures without imposing even the most minimal reforms. The Italian army high command resisted modern technology. It understood that it could not take on France or Britain in any major war. Colonial wars and potential conflict with Yugoslavia did not demand a serious rethinking of modernization. The military shared Mussolini's belief in numbers over machines and technology. Italy opted for as large an army as possible but one, while rich in number of officers, was deficient in modern equipment from tanks to radios and radar. Even as Italy allied with Nazi Germany and embarked on an extremely risky foreign policy, the Italian military establishment was slow to change. The navy and air force were more open to technology but by the late 1930s the army remained essentially what it had been after the First World War. Thus, the Italian idea of 'rapid warfare' was as different from the German blitzkrieg as mules and marching soldiers were different from mobile Panzer divisions.

From the start, the German military had a central place in Hitler's priorities. The Führer and his army initially agreed on two goals: the perpetuation of the Army's autonomous status within the power structure of the state, and the reassertion of German power through rapid rearmament. But the German generals' ability to protect the old Prussian traditions of autonomy was undermined by a number of changes that had taken place after the First World War. The army imposed by the Versailles treaty was limited to 100,000 men and the officer corps was restricted to around 3,000 officers. As a result the military establishment tended to close in around itself. Over half of military cadets were sons of officers in the early 1930s and one-quarter were from the nobility. With the rapid rearmament under the Nazis this officer corps dramatically altered. By 1938 it had risen to 21,700 and by the outbreak of the war the military had 89,075 regular and reserve officers.[2] Unlike Fascist Italy where Mussolini did not interfere in the traditional system of military promotions, by the late 1930s most German officers owed their positions directly to Hitler. The German army was also much more open to innovation and to modern technology than its Italian counterpart. Many new officers rose from the NCO ranks, not as in Italy on formal education or connections, but on talent and the ability to produce results.

The German army shared much common ground with Hitler and the Nazi leadership. The military leaders and the Führer did not diverge either on the need for an authoritarian solution to Germany's political crisis or the need to reassert the nation's status as a great power. Both the military and the Nazis emerged from the 'trench generation' of the First World War. They shared a common reference system and values. The Italian military never fully identified with the ideology of the regime as did the German generals. One example among many will suffice. On 10 October 1941 Field Marshal von Richenau, commander of the Sixth Army on the eastern front wrote:

> The essential goal of the campaign against the Jewish–Bolshevik system is the complete destruction of its power instruments and the eradication of the Asiatic influence on the European cultural sphere. Therefore the troops too have tasks which go beyond the conventional soldierly tradition. In the east the soldier is not only a fighter but also a carrier of an inexorable racial conception and the avenger of all the bestialities which have been committed against the Germans and related races.[3]

Italian officers for all their faults would have had a hard time writing such drivel.

When the two regimes were put to the test of war in 1939 and 1940, the contrasts between Fascist Italy and Nazi Germany proved fatal for Italian regime. The Axis was an alliance that operated in two totally different military worlds. Once again, the Italian regime proved unable to escape from the compromises it made during the consolidation of power phase. Mussolini's style of governing only made things worse.

14 Imperialism and expansion
The Fascist and Nazi regimes
and the challenge of war

Historians have debated whether the direction taken by Fascist and Nazi regimes was dictated by the ideology or will of the supreme leader or whether it was more the outcome of institutional forces interacting within the framework of the dictatorships. The intentionalist position is stronger in questions of foreign policy than it is in domestic policy. The fascist style of rule became a system of collective irresponsibility that gave to the Duce and Führer enormous latitude in the conduct of international relations. Multiple power centres, competing in an ill-defined and evolving constitutional framework, left both Mussolini and Hitler as the ultimate arbiters over foreign policy, which fell outside of the sphere of control any single or combination of domestic constituencies. As we have seen, constitutional and political controls were extremely weak in any case and in foreign policy they came more from the European balance of power than from forces inside the regimes.

On coming to power, Hitler had to initiate a policy of rearmament, then remilitarize the Rhineland, before he could act aggressively in Europe. Similarly, Fascist Italy during the 1920s and early 1930s found itself in a weak position to challenge either France or Britain. Mussolini's goal of domination of the Mediterranean Sea and the establishment of an Italian imperial sphere from the Balkans to East Africa and from Suez to Gibraltar needed the favourable international context provided by the rise of Nazi Germany.

A full analysis of the expansionist aims of the two dictators is beyond the scope of this brief work, which is more devoted to internal policy, but a few general considerations are possible. Fascist Italy and Nazi Germany both broke free from the limits on their ambitions in foreign policy at about the same time. Mussolini's decision for war in Ethiopia, taken in 1934 and carried out at the end of 1935, led to a rupture with Britain and France. His subsequent involvement in the Spanish Civil War in July 1936 sealed the break with the western democracies and offered the chance to realize his imperial ambitions in alliance with Nazi Germany. Hitler freed Germany from the constraints of the Versailles Treaty in March 1936, when he sent his army into the demilitarized Rhineland and pushed his defensive frontier to the borders of France and Belgium. Both dictators acted against the advice of their military establishments. Vindication by subsequent events gave both men a feeling of omnipotence and made them less willing to listen to the advice of experts when taking major decisions.[1] Emboldened by the belief that history was on their side, Hitler and Mussolini took a much more radical and aggressive direction in both foreign and domestic policy after 1936. Imperialist expansion, a renewed push for totalitarian control internally and a turning of the screws on the issue of race were linked, as Hitler and Mussolini sought to remake the domestic and international political order. A number of recent studies of Fascist foreign policy reveal a Duce who took greater and greater risks, rejected overtures from Britain for better relations and used the German alliance to his advantage as he strove for domination in the Mediterranean region.[2] Even though the Duce understood by 1938 that the Italian military would not be ready for a general European war until after 1942, he continued, almost deliberately, to make a conflict more and more likely.

Italy entered the Second World War completely unprepared. The contrast between the two regimes was no more apparent than in the way they collapsed. War was immediately fatal for Mussolini's regime, whereas the Nazi state held up under the pressures of a two-front war. It is a sad commentary on the pretentions and bombast of fascism that, after almost seventeen years of rule, fourteen of which were without opposition, Italy was less prepared morally, economically and politically for war in 1939 and 1940 that it had been in 1915 under the much-maligned liberal government. The Italian debacle of late 1940 and early 1941 went beyond questions of leadership to involve an entire system that had lost all sense of dynamism.[3]

When the Duce actually joined the German war against France on 10 June 1940, the Fascist government acted on the belief that

Germany had already won the war. After months of hesitation, Mussolini feared that he might be absent from the peace negotiations and would enjoy few of the fruits of victory. Like the Führer, the Duce had always de-emphasized economic or military factors in favour of his broad political, ideological and diplomatic strategy. Both dictators translated the primacy of the political and ideological into a short-term programme of successful military aggression from 1935 to 1940.[4] A policy predicated on rapid and easy victories was also structurally compatible with regimes that sought to avoid the creation of an economic and military power centre that might threaten the position of the supreme leader.[5] Therefore, in light of the certain German victory of June 1940, Italy's alarming lack of preparation did not seem to matter.[6]

Mussolini believed that he could carve out a sphere of influence in the Balkans and in the Mediterranean while his more powerful ally conquered England and France, This 'parallel war' theory rested on the assumption that Germany would remain outside of the Italian sphere of interest in the Mediterranean and the Balkan regions and that Italy alone could deal with England in North Africa and Yugoslavia and Greece in the Balkans. But to do this, the Italians had to win military victories with an army that was hopelessly inadequate. Only after it won control of resources in the Balkans would its supply situation improve. In a sense, this concept was a poor copy of the Nazi *Grossraumwirtschaft*, the economy of territorial conquest to overcome deficiencies. But the Germans had mobilized and planned for decisive short-run victories, while the Italians just assumed their superiority over Greece. Once Greek resistance made a mockery of fascism's military pretensions in October and November 1940, the parallel war collapsed and Italy was left with no alternative but to appeal for German assistance in early 1941.

The war revealed the residual strength of the various conservative constituencies that had rallied behind Italian fascism but had not completely wedded their fate to that of the regime. Even the monarchy and the military were able, successfully in the short term, to step back from their twenty-year embrace of the dictatorship. Important industrialists, the Catholic hierarchy and many intellectuals found it even easier to disengage psychologically from the regime in 1942 and 1943. When the regime dissolved, each constituent element had preserved something of its original base, which it could use as a springboard to the post-fascist era.[7]

A similar strategy was not possible in Nazi Germany for several reasons. The decision, taken by the Allies at Casablanca in early 1943, to impose unconditional surrender on Germany meant that there was less possibility for negotiations between the Allied Powers and remnants of the German conservative elites. Italy, considered a secondary enemy, was allowed to negotiate a separate peace under a government that had strong continuity with the old Fascist regime. But the differences between Italy and Germany went deeper than that. Both regimes determined to mobilize the population psychologically and physically for war, but the Nazis accomplished much more than the Fascists. In Germany after 1936 the power of the traditional elites diminished as Germany directed its energies into war, and that of the various party formations, such as the SS, grew. Neither regime had significant opposition from their military establishments after 1936. Hitler assumed overall command of the Army after the 1938 crisis, which resulted in the dismissal of Blomberg and Fritsch. In those same years, Mussolini nominally held the War, Air and Navy Ministries. But the Nazi regime's propensity to create new parallel administrations for economic, security and racial policy pushed aside the old civil service. In Italy, where political repression was in the hands of the state bureaucracy, older prefascist values and loyalties could reassert themselves when it became clear that the Fascist system was collapsing. Part of the state apparatus eventually combined with Fascist dissidents and supporters of the monarchy to topple Mussolini.

Conclusion

Throughout this volume, I have attempted to point out similarities and significant differences between the Fascist and Nazi regimes. Both were part of a generic fascist style of governing. The Fascist and Nazi movements developed out of the same social, political, and cultural crisis of post-First World War Europe. Both regimes consciously envisaged themselves not only as a response to the crisis of liberalism in an age of mass politics, but also as alternatives to the Bolshevik model of organizing society on the basis of class. The Fascists proposed unity on the basis of an organic nation; the Nazis did the same on the basis of racial biology, but, as we have seen, by the late 1930s the conceptions often differed more in degree than in fundamental principles. Both national communities would be made homogeneous by a radical purge of unwanted elements. Finally, both regimes stressed the primacy of politics over economics and expansion over stability in the final phase of their existence.

Despite their claims to represent the entire nation, fascism and nazism were ideologies of bourgeois resurgence, at least in their initial stages. Italian fascism remained so until the end despite Mussolini's determination to change it. I do not intend to argue that the two regimes were puppets of great industry and finance. There was certainly a mismatch between the desires of the conservative and bourgeois constituencies that backed the Fascists and the Nazis on their march to power and the aims and ideology of Mussolini, Hitler and their close associates. Nonetheless, the policies pursued by both regimes tended to reinforce existing social and gender hierarchies. This reactionary tendency was quite apparent in economic, family, gender and educational policy.

Acceptance of the existing economic structures and class divisions had important consequences. The Fascist and Nazi leadership had to work with and around the established social and economic elites even after they stabilized power. The system of government that they created reflected these limitations. The old political system, already in crisis in both Italy and Germany after the war, was gutted or allowed to fall into disuse without creating a new, permanent order. Constitutional and administrative practice was improvised on a daily basis as deals were made between the Fascist and Nazi leaders and key interest groups in the state, party and private economy to carve out areas of political and economic power. The notion that these regimes were socially or economically revolutionary was compromised from the outset but remained powerful propaganda themes until the end.

While the fascist style was not always the same in Italy and Germany, many of the differences were more in execution than in intent. The Nazi regime was certainly on a higher level of economic development and had a much stronger state apparatus. Nonetheless, each came to offer a totalitarian vision of a new society in which a fusion between the private and the collective or the individual and the mass would take place. For instance, we have seen that in both regimes the notion of 'free' professions or apolitical intellectuals was flatly rejected. At least in theory, each individual in all aspects of life would be integrated into the state. On the other side of the ledger, the persistence of compromises with the old social, religious and economic establishment in Italy and the relative strength of the state apparatus in each country clearly affected outcome of the totalitarian project.

The structure of both regimes tended to distort and mute ideology; ideology, in turn, offered a constant measure by which the regimes could aspire to vaster political, social and economic change. In Fascist Italy the structural problems and compromises with the old order sapped the regime's revolutionary pretensions throughout the twenty-one years of rule; Nazi racial ideology and the Führer's anarchic way of running the state rendered the German regime more dynamic but also more radical and unstable. Racial ideology infused nazism with a unique, almost revolutionary, vision. The Nazis were able to apply this racial principle to the world of culture, science and even to economic and social relations, with devastating effect. Moreover in Nazi Germany the racial mission penetrated deeply into the bureaucratic apparatus. Ian Kershaw cited one Nazi mid-level official Arthur Greiser in May 1942, who justified his order to execute 35,000 Poles:

> I myself do not believe that the Führer needs to be asked again in this matter, especially since at our last discussion with regard to the Jews, he told me that I could proceed with these according to my own judgement.[1]

In Fascist Italy, on matters of race but also on many other things after 1938, the bureaucracy had little desire to push to a radical conclusion. Italians were not 'working toward the Duce' with anything like the dedication that the Nazis brought. But even an inept, bungling and unenthusiastic regime managed to do much harm to Italian and foreign Jews from 1938 to 1943.[2]

The power of the Catholic Church was such that certain measures, not so much against the Jews who were not a high priority for the Vatican, but dealing with sterilization and euthanasia, could not be taken in Italy. But there were those within the Fascist movement who wanted to follow the Nazi path; Fascist ideology offered precious little defence against whatever direction Mussolini wanted to take. What stopped the Fascists was not their inherently good 'Italian' character, but a series of structural and institutional limitations that frustrated radical and racial versions of fascism after 1936, even as Mussolini sought to remove them as he edged toward war on the side of Hitler.

Thus, the fundamental difference between the Nazi and Fascist regimes was the strength of the traditional order. The Fascists operated in a society based on religious and social structures that were much stronger than the state apparatus. The Fascists made initial compromises that were never undone. With the Lateran Treaty and the Concordat of 1929 Mussolini's regime was forced to accommodate the equally 'total' claims of the Catholic Church. During the 1930s the Church burrowed into the structures of the regime from the operations of the Balilla organization to the reconversion to Catholicism of part of the political class. Similarly the monarchy, though constantly in retreat, maintained its own rituals and hierarchies separate from those of the regime. Mussolini's bargain with the military meant that he could shape overall foreign and military policy but not the instrument needed to carry out those policies. In large parts of the South, the Fascist state continued to be relatively weak with respect to the Church and the landed elites.

Italian fascism in the early 1930s might have moved in the direction eventually taken by Franco's Spain – an authoritarian extremely stable repressive regime, but Mussolini deliberately abandoned that path in 1935 and 1936. The radical Fascists of the younger generation hoped that a revived Fascist revolution could be achieved on the imperial level or with victory in war. If it had come with the Second World War, it would have taken place in the context of a Nazi-dominated Europe where restraints imposed by the traditional conservative order would certainly have been less effective.

The Nazis were more free, if never entirely liberated, from any such institutional constraints as they moved into a second stage of fascist-style rule. In the area of public discourse, Nazi symbols, rituals and hierarchies had no competition from the conservative establishment. Organized religion acted as an occasional brake when the Nazis trampled on bedrock beliefs of the countryside or when otherwise quiescent clerymen, like the Archbishop von Galen of Munster, spoke out against the euthanasia program. Religious resistance was relegated more to the realm of private conscience. Industry and the military were integrated into the Four Year Plan and mobilization for war. The initial foreign policy successes of Hitler after 1936 silenced any doubters. The shift of power to organizations affiliated with the Nazi party or with key party officials (Himmler with the police and the SS, Göring with the Four Year Plan and his gigantic holding company) figured prominently in this second stage that had only a weak counterpart in Fascist Italy.

In the area of culture, striking differences existed between the Fascist and Nazi regimes. That this was so is again attributable to the strength of the conservative order within fascism. The various fiefdoms within the framework of the Fascist state carved out their own territory and set their own cultural agendas. In contrast, after the shock of defeat in the First World War and the identification of the avant-garde with the hated Weimar Republic, the conservative order in Germany was less willing to extend its protection to 'subversive' art. The Nazi regime lacked any connections with modernist artistic movements, such as existed between the Fascists and futurism or the Novecento movement. Even before the Nazi state managed to liberate itself from the compromises that brought it to power, it began the purge of culture under the guise of ridding Germany of cosmopolitan Judeo-Bolshevism.

The National Socialist regime developed its own version of the fascist-style of rule that gave a greater role to a party-dominated para-state sector in the economy and internal security. The composition of and balance within the fiefdoms differed but the basic structure remained the same. If the power of the private industrial cartels *vis-à-vis* the state diminished in Nazi Germany and the influence of the Church was nowhere near as great, these power centres did not completely disappear or lose influence. In both states a substantial part of the traditional social, cultural and economic structure survived the dictatorship, war and defeat to emerge in the postwar era. Certainly, state continuity, in terms of personnel and institutions, seemed much more pronounced between the Fascist regime and the postwar Italian Republic. From the failure of the purge of Fascist collaborators to the continued existence of the IRI, the Dopolavoro, the Rocco legal codes and the Lateran Treaty, aspects of the Fascist regime lived on well into the Republic. On the face of it, much less of the Nazi system survived. But the Nazi regime simply did not last very long and many of the institutions that it created were intrinsically connected to war and conquest. In contrast, the economic institutions of fascism were a response to the Great Depression or to structural weaknesses in the economy and could be adapted by the postwar governments. It is exceedingly difficult to determine how many of the changes in village and small town life that have been attributed to the Nazi regime were actually brought about by war, the massive bombardment of the country and the subsequent defeat and foreign occupation. Eastern Germany fell within the Soviet zone. There the landed elites lost their property. Vast population movements from east to west, a more vigorous process of denazification and a prolonged period of foreign occupation produced a more profound sense of rupture. However, the extent of change should not be exaggerated. Adenauer's Germany after 1949 carried over a good part of the private and public sector personnel from the Nazi years.[3]

I might conclude with a last observation. When I wrote the first edition of my survey of the Fascist regime, *Fascist Italy: Its Origins and Development*, in 1982, I was convinced that fascism and nazism were two distinct phenomena. Over the years this conviction has changed. While I have not tried to force the two regimes into a rigid model, I do believe that they share many things in common. It has been (and still is) extremely convenient on the Italian side to distinguish the Fascist regime sharply from the Nazi variant. This tendency has led to a greater willingness to allow fascism back within the great national tent. The Fascist regime lasted over twenty years, much longer than its Nazi counterpart, and involved directly or indirectly almost the entire country in its operation, as the failure of the postwar purges in Italy makes clear.

Fascism and nazism were regimes that operated on principles that were antithetical to liberal values. On any scale, their core beliefs were much closer to each other than to liberal or social democracy. As we incorporate the fascist experience within the historical development of Italy and Germany, the moral and ideological line of demarcation between the values of liberal Italy before 1922 and of republican Italy after 1945 or between Weimar and the later Federal Republic of Germany and the principles on which fascism and nazism rested needs to be made clear. One occasionally hears the argument that Mussolini's regime might have been a positive force if it had not gone astray after 1938 or that Hitler might have been a great leader if he had only stopped after putting the Germans back to work and not gone to war and murdered so many Jews. But the outcome of the two regimes cannot be separated from the way they seized power, from the principles that inspired their ideology, from the way they treated opponents, and from the style of rule that they adopted once power was achieved. The Fascist and Nazi regimes are fundamentally linked, not just in historical time but on a deeper level. For a historian writing in a democratic or liberal tradition, to ask when the two regimes or their leaders went wrong is to put the issue badly. The simple answer is, from the beginning to the end.

Notes

Introduction

1 Three works reflect this trend: Richard Bessel (ed.), *Fascist Italy and Nazi Germany: Comparisons and Contrasts* (Cambridge, 1996); Aristotle A. Kallis, *Fascist Ideology: Territory and Expansionism in Italy and Germany, 1922–1945* (London and New York, 2000); MacGregor Knox, *Common Destiny: Dictatorship, Foreign Policy and War in Fascist Italy and Nazi Germany* (Cambridge, 2000). Three slightly older works are also important: Paul Booker, *Faces of Fraternalism: Nazi Germany, Fascist Italy and Imperial Japan* (Oxford, 1991) and Roger Griffin, *The Nature of Fascism* (New York, 1991); and Karl Dietrich Bracher and Leo Valiani, *Fascismo e nazionalsocialismo* (Bologna, 1986).

2 In addition to the work of Roger Griffin, see Roger Eatwell, *Fascism: A History* (London, 1996); Stanley Payne, *A History of Fascism, 1914–1945* (Madison, 1995); Robert O. Paxton, 'The Five Stages of Fascism', *Journal of Modern History* 70 (1998) (1) 1–23. For an excellent introduction to the evolution of the debate on fascism, see Aristotle Kallis's introduction to *The Fascism Reader* (London, 2003). My own views are probably closer to those like Robert Soucy who see fascism in Italy and France as an essentially conservative movement that failed to disturb existing social and economic hierarchies. This would be true despite efforts by Mussolini to break free from compromises with the established order. See Robert Soucy, *French Fascism: The Second Wave 1933–1939* (New Haven, 1995). This work has been revised in a new French edition, *Fascismes françaises 1933–1939: Mouvements antidémocratiques* (Paris, 2004).

3 See Meir Michaelis, 'Fascism, Totalitarianism and the Holocaust: Reflexions on Current Interpretations of National Socialist Anti-Semitism', *European History Quarterly* 19 (1989) 85–103; Abbott Gleason, *Totalitarianism: The Inner History of the Cold War* (Oxford, 1995); and, most importantly, the work of Emilio Gentile, *La via italiana al totalitarismo. Il partito e lo stato nel regime fascista* (Rome, 1995).

4 Ian Kershaw, *Hitler: 1889–1936: Hubris* (New York, 1998) and *Hitler 1936–1945: Nemesis* (New York and London, 2000); Richard J. B. Bosworth, *Mussolini* (London, 2002).

5 On the presence of workers in the Nazi movement, see Detlef Mühlberger, *Hitler's Followers: Studies in the Sociology of the Nazi Movement* (London and New York, 1991), but the author concedes that:

> The Nazi party was, as the Nazis themselves asserted in the 1920s and 1930s, a *Volkspartei*, a mass movement in which all classes were represented. This is not to ignore the fact that the sociological structure of the NSDAP, the SA, and the SS mirrored the social composition of German society imperfectly, either at the macro or micro level. The lower- and middle-middle class and elite were over-represented and the lower class under-represented within the NSDAP and the SS before 1933 . . . The characterization of the Nazi Movement as a *Volkspartei* does need to be qualified, however. It was a predominantly male affair on the one hand, and primarily a movement of the younger age groups of German society on the other.
>
> (p. 207)

On the social composition of the Fascist movement, see Jens Petersen, 'Elettorato e base sociale del fascismo italiano negli anni venti', *Studi storici* 16 (1975), 627–9; Juan Linz, 'Some notes toward a comparative study of fascism in a sociological historical perspective', in Walter Lacqueur (ed.), *Fascism: A Reader's Guide* (Berkeley, 1976).

6 On Nazi Germany as a 'polycracy', see Martin Broszat, *The Hitler State: The Foundation and Development of the Internal Structure of the Third Reich* (London, 1981); Hans Mommsen, *Beamtentum in Dritten Reich* (Stuttgart, 1966); Robert Koehl, 'Feudal Aspects of National Socialism', *American Political Science Review* 54 (1960) 921–33. I tried to use a similar approach in studying Italian fascism, *Italian Fascism: Its Origins and Development* (3rd edn, Lincoln, Nebraska, 2000).

1 Fascism and nazism before the seizure of power

1 Italy refinanced its debt from notes bearing as much as 5 per cent interest to issues at 3 per cent and 3.5 per cent. For the impact of the crisis of 1907, see Franco Bonelli, *La crisi del 1907* (Turin, 1971).

2 Angelo Tasca's *Rise of Italian Fascism* (New York, 1966) is still a fine survey of the Fascist onslaught.

3 See Detlev Peukert, *The Weimar Republic* (New York, 1989), pp. 87–91; Richard Overy, *War and Economy in the Third Reich* (Oxford, 1994), p. 38. For a striking picture of this generational disorientation, see Hans Fallada's *Little Man, What Now* (Chicago, 1983).

4 On the breakdown of the Weimar social consensus, see David Abraham, *The Collapse of the Weimar Republic,* 2nd edn (New York and London, 1986).

2 The rise of fascism and nazism

1 On the problem of Fascist modernism, see Jeffrey Herf, *Reactionary Modernism* (Cambridge, 1984); Dagmar Barnouw, *Weimar Intellectuals and the Threat of Modernity* (Bloomington, IL, 1988); Andrew Hewitt, *Fascist Modernism* (Stanford, 1993); Walter Adamson, *Avant-garde Florence* (Cambridge, MA, 1993); Modris Eksteins, *Rites of Spring: The Great War and the Birth of the Modern Age* (New York, 1989); the catalogue of the Paris exhibit, *Les realismes 1919–1939* (Paris, 1981).

2 Sternhell may overstate the importance of anti-Semitism in separating fascism from nazism. There was a racist core to fascism that could be turned towards anti-Semitism under the right circumstances. Clearly, the ideology itself presented no obstacles. On the origins of fascism, see Emilio Gentile, *Gli origini dell'ideologia fascista* (Bari, 1975); Walter Adamson, *Avant-garde Florence* and Sternhell, *The Birth of Fascist Ideology.* For the links between Mussolini and this Franco-Italian tradition, see Renzo De Felice, *Mussolini il rivoluzionario* (Turin, 1965) and A. James Gregor, *Young Mussolini and the Intellectual Origins of Fascism* (Berkeley, 1979).

3 On Mussolini's state of mind in 1917 and 1918, see Renzo De Felice, *Mussolini il rivoluzionario,* Chapter 11, especially p. 406.

4 See Max Kele, *Nazis and Workers: National Socialist Appeals to* German Labor, *1919–1933* (Chapel Hill, 1972). Mühlberger has offered another model to analyse lower-class support for the Nazis. He noted that only 1.3 million workers belonged to the SPD or KPD and 'only approximately half of the 22 to 25 million workers and their adult dependants gave their electoral support to the socialist and marxist parties in the late 1920s and early 1930s'. Even if the Catholic workers are included, Mühlberger concludes that there was a significant mass of workers outside of the established parties who could be drawn to the Nazis in the late 1920s and early 1930s. It was likely that they were younger, unorganized, small-town workers. See *Hitler's Followers,* pp. 203–5.

5 The Fascists faced their generational problem during the regime itself when the relatively young political establishment of the 1920s reached the late 1930s with no signs of a changing of the guard. On the generational problem, see Robert Wohl, *Generation of 1914* (Cambridge, MA, 1979); Peter Gay, *Weimar Culture* (New York. 1968); D. Dowe (ed.), *Jugendprotest und Generationskonflikt in Europa im 20 Jahrhundert* (Bonn, 1986); Michael Kater, 'Generationskonflikt als Entwicklungsfaktor in der NS-Bewegung vor 1933', *Geschichte und Gesellschaft,* 11 (1985), 217–43; Luisa Mangoni, *L'interventismo della cultura* (Bari, 1974).

3   The march to power

1 Historians such as Renzo De Felice and Emilio Gentile in Italy and A. James Gregor in the United States have stressed the importance and persistence of Mussolini's socialism throughout his political life, See De Felice, *Mussolini it rivoluzionario* and A. James Gregor, *Young Mussolini and the Intellectual Origins of Fascism*. For a contrasting view, see Denis Mack Smith, *Mussolini* (London, 1980) and Roberto Vivarelli, *Storia delle origini del fascismo*, vol. 1 *Dalla fine della guerra all'impresa di Fiume* (Naples, 1967), and vol. 2 *L'Italia dalla grande guerra alla marcia su Roma* (Bologna, 1991).

2 Jens Peterson, 'Elettorato e base sociale del fascismo italiano negli anni venti', *Studi storici*, 16 (1975) 655–7, for the analysis of party membership.

3 No one has carried out an analysis for Italy similar to Klaus Theweleit's *Male Fantasies* (2 vols) (Minneapolis, 1987). Theweleit studied the particular male bonding, fear of and hostility to women, and the vicious hatred of Communism among the Freikorps veterans. There has been a considerable literature on the connection between the wartime spirit and the Fascist squads. See Luisa Mangoni, *L'interventismo nella cultura: Intellettuali e riviste del fascismo* (Bari, 1974), and Mario Isnenghi, *Il mito della grande guerra* (Bari, 1970).

4 Theweleit noted that some Freikorps, who were too young to see action in the war, found their redemption in the civil war against the socialists and Communists in 1919 and 1920. As the Freikorps units dissolved, the veterans spread throughout many far right movements. The process was accelerated after the failure of the November 1923 Munich *putsch* against the Weimar Republic (Theweleit, vol. I, 24–5). The same phenomenon existed in Italy, although the battle was over in 1922 and the generation that missed the war had only limited opportunities after the March on Rome. Unlike the Fascist squads, the composition of the SA in the late 1920s and early 1930s came to include a large number of younger, unemployed lower-class males.

5 See *Mein Kampf* (London, 1941), p. 479, cited in Tim Mason, *Social Policy in the Third Reich: The Working Class and the National Community* (Providence and Oxford, 1993), p. 47.

6 Michael Kater noted that the Nazis managed to emerge with at least one seat in sixteen of the thirty Landtag and Reichstag elections from 1925 until the mid-1930s. See Michael Kater, *The Nazi Party* (Cambridge, MA, 1983), p. 49.

7 The stress on solidarity or fraternalism is emphasized by Paul Brooker. Brooker argued that it offered a broader vision than other movements could present. See Brooker, *Faces of Fraternalism*, Chapter 1.

8 Peukert, *The Weirnar Republic*, p. 239.

9 On the formalization of the relations between the Fascist groups and agrarians in Emilia in the winter of 1921, see Anthony Cardoza,

Agrarian Elites and Italian Fascism: The Province of Bologna 1901–1926 (Princeton, 1982), pp. 323–39; Paul Corner, *Il fascismo a Ferrara* (Bari,1974), Chapter 7; Alice Kelikian, *Town and Country under Fascism: The Transformation of Brescia 1915–1926* (Oxford, 1986), pp. 144–53. Kelikian notes that the local industrialists were much less willing to ally with the *fasci* than were the landowners.

10 See Paul Hayes, *Industry and Ideology: I. G. Farben in the Nazi Era* (Cambridge, 1987), pp. 57–61 on financial ties between the I.G. Farben and its top executives and the conservatives in 1930–2. On Krupp, see Richard Overy, 'Primacy Always Belongs to Politics: Gustav Krupp and the Third Reich', in *War and Economy in the Third Reich*, pp. 119–43, especially p. 127. See also Henry Ashby Turner, *German Big Business and the Rise of Hitler* (New York, 1985) for a thorough and convincing account of the financing of the Nazi movement.

11 Tim Mason, *Social Policy in the Third Reich*, p. 42.

4 The exercise of power

1 On the general economic conditions at the moment of the transition, see Harold James, *The German Slump: Politics and Economics 1924–1936* (Oxford, 1986) and Douglas Forsyth, *The Crisis of Liberal Italy: Monetary and Financial Policy, 1914–1922* (Cambridge, 1993).

2 The Acerbo Law created a single national college but allowed for regional lists. Unlike the single member district that exists in the United Kingdom and the American House of Representatives, the voter does not elect a specific candidate. The winners are not decided by the first past the post rule but by percentages of voters. Under the Acerbo Law the one-third of opposition seats were so assigned. The government sponsored National List was made up of 275 Fascists and ninety-nine fellow travellers. Opposition and independent lists won roughly one-third of the 7.2 million votes cast. For an election analysis, see Christopher Seton-Watson, *Italy from Liberalism to Fascism* (London, 1967), pp. 648–9.

3 See Hans Mommsen, 'The Reichstag Fire and its Political Consequences', in H, W. Koch (ed.), *Aspects of the Third Reich* (Basingstoke, 1985).

4 The weakness of the Fascists and Nazis in urban areas accentuated the fears of the two leaders over the loyalty of the urban masses. During the military buildup of the 1930s and for the first years of the Second World War, the Nazis and Fascists pursued a policy of guns *and* butter. See Broszat, *Hitler State*, p. 76, Table 3.1, and Adrian Lyttelton, *The Seizure of Power* (New York, 1973), p. 146.

5 On the extent of the purges, see Jane Caplan, *Government Without Administration: State and Civil Service in Weimar and Nazi Germany* (Oxford, 1988), p. 145, and Alberto Aquarone, *L'organizzazione dello Stato totalitario* (Turin, 1965), pp. 74–5.

5   The new order

1 Jeremy Noakes and Geoffrey Pridham (eds), *Nazism 1919–1945: State, Economy and Society 1933–1939* (vol. 2) (Exeter, 1984), p. 245.

2 On the debate over Hitler, see Ian Kershaw, *The Nazi Dictatorship: Problems and Perspectives of Interpretation* (3rd edn, London, 1993), Chapter 4, and Richard Overy, 'Hitler's War Plans and the German Economy, 1933–1939', in *War and Economy in the Third Reich*, pp. 178–204.

3 Ian Kershaw, 'Working toward the Führer: Reflections on the Nature of the Hitler Dictatorship', in Christian Leitz (ed.), *The Third Reich: The Essential Readings* (Oxford, 1999), p. 245. Evidence of a similar radicalization can be found in Italy after 1936. See Alexander De Grand, 'Mussolini's Follies: Italian Fascism in its Imperial and Racist Phase, 1935–1940', *Contemporary European History*, 13 (2004) 127–47.

4 This case is analysed in Philip Morgan, *Fascism in Europe 1919–1945* (London, 2003), pp. 137–8

5 Scorza to Mussolini, 7 June 1943, cited in Renzo De Felice, *Mussolini l'alleato: L'Italia in guerra 1940–1943* (part 1) (Turin, 1990), p. 1001. Robert Koehl analyzed the systems of alliances, peace treaties and mediation among Nazi leaders. See 'Feudal Aspects of National Socialism', in Henry A. Turner (ed.), *Nazism and the Third Reich* (New York 1982), p. 160.

6 Kershaw, 'Working toward the Führer', in Leitz, *The Third Reich*, p. 241.

6   The institutionalization of the party

1 Pierre Ayçoberry, *A Social History of the Third Reich, 1933–1945* (New York, 1999), p. 86.

2 See Caplan, *Government without Administration*, p. 219; for Italy, see also Aquarone, *L'organizzazione dello stato totalitario*, p. 186.

7   The Fascist and Nazi economic systems

1 On the general question of Fascism and Nazism and the economy, see for Italy Piero Melograni, *Gli industriali e Mussolini* (Milan, 1972) and Roland Sarti, *Fascism and the Industrial Leadership in Italy* (Berkeley, 1971): and for Germany, Berenice Carroll, *Design for Total War: Arms and Economics in the Third Reich* (The Hague, 1968); Richard J. Overy, *The Nazi Economic Recovery 1932–1938* (London, 1982); John R. Gillingham, *Industry and Politics in the Third Reich: Ruhr Coal, Hitler and Europe* (New York, 1985); Avarham Barkai, *Nazi Economics: Ideology, Theory, and Policy* (New Haven, 1990).

2 On the elimination of the NSBO and the German Labour Front from collective bargaining by the Law for Regulation of National Labour of January 1934, see Barkai, *Nazi Economics*, pp. 122–8. Barkai also notes

continuing jurisdictional disputes between Ley's organization and other ministries.

3 Ayçoberry, *The Social History of the Third Reich 1933–1945*, p. 148.

4 On the negative impact of Fascist food policies, especially as Italy moved to a war footing and an alliance with Nazi Germany, see Carol F. Helstosky, 'Fascist Food Politics: Mussolini's Policy of Alimentary sovereignty', *Journal of Modern Italian Studies* 9 (Spring 2004), 1–26.

5 J. E. Farquharson, *The Plough and the Swastika: The NSDAP and Agriculture 1928–1945* (London and Beverley Hills, 1976), p. 11.

8 Autarky and economic mobilization

1 Broszat, *Nazi State*, p. 172.

2 Caplan, *Government without Administration*, p. 153–4.

3 See Peter Hayes, *Industry and Ideology*, p. 77.

4 Richard Overy, *Göring: The 'Iron Man'* (London, 1984), p. 50, and 'Heavy Industry in the Third Reich: The Reichswerke Crisis', in *War and Economy in the Third Reich*, pp. 93–118.

9 The new 'fascist' community: demography and race

1 On the German side, see Michael Burleigh, *The Third Reich: A New History* (New York, 2000); Götz Aly, *The Final Solution: Nazi Population Policy and the Murder of the European Jews* (London and New York, 1999); Claudia Koonz, *The Nazi Conscience* (Cambridge, MA, 2003). From the perspective of Italy, see Michele Sarfatti, *Gli ebrei nell'Italia fascista: Vicende, identità, persecuzione* (Turin, 2000); Giorgio Israel and Pietro Nastasi, *Scienza e razza nell'Italia fascista* (Bologna, 1998); Roberto Maiocchi, *Scienza italiana e razzismo fascista* (Florence, 1999); Carl Ipsen, *Dictating Demography: The Problem of Populaton in Fascist Italy* (Cambridge, 1996); Gabriele Turi, *Lo Stato educatore: Politica e intellettuali nell'Italia fascista* (Bari, 2002).

2 See Hannah Arendt, *The Origins of Totalitarianism: Imperialism* (part 2) (New York, 1968), Chapter 5 'The Decline of the Nation-State and the End of the Rights of Man', especially pp. 170–82.

3 Jill Stephenson, *Women in Nazi Society* (New York, 1975), p. 37.

4 Victoria De Grazia, *How Fascism Ruled Women* (Berkeley, 1992), p. 181.

5 Claudia Koonz cites a 1936 SS report that estimated that 500,000 had been performed; other estimates ranged up to 1 million annually. Figures like these raise questions about the true impact of the totalitarian state in the private sphere. See Claudia Koonz, *Mothers in the Fatherland: Women, the Family, and Nazi Politics* (New York, 1987), pp. 186–7. Italian estimates on abortion were also quite high; See Denise Detragiache, 'Un aspect de la politique demographique de l'Italie fasciste: La repression de l'avortement', *Mélanges de l'École française de*

Rome (1980), 690–732. An excellent treatment of racial policy as it affected marriage, abortion, sterilization and euthanasia in Nazi Germany is Michael Burleigh's and Wolfgang Wippermann's *The Racial State: Germany 1933–1945* (Cambridge, 1991), especially Chapter 3.

6 Claudia Koonz, *The Nazi Conscience* (Cambridge, MA, 2003), pp. 169–72.

7 Koonz, *The Nazi Conscience*, pp. 185–9

8 Koonz, *The Nazi Conscience*, p. 197.

9 Götz Aly, 'The Planning Intelligentsia and the "Final Solution"', in Michael Burleigh (ed.), *Confronting the Nazi Past: New Debates on Modern German History* (New York, 1996), pp. 140–1.

10 Victor Klemperer, *I Will Bear Witness 1942–1945: A Diary of the Nazi Years* (New York, 2001), entry for 2 June 1942, pp. 64–6.

11 Roberto Maiocchi, *Scienza italiana e razzismo fascista* (Florence, 1999), p. 210.

12 Gabriele Turi, *Lo Stato educatore: Politica e intellettuali nell'Italia fascista* (Bari–Rome, 2002), p. 126.

13 Turi, *Lo Stato educatore*, p. 135.

14 Turi, *Lo Stato educatore*, p. 122. In December, 400 teachers of various grades were expelled from the universities.

15 Enso Collotti and Lutz Klinkhammer, *Il fascismo e l'Italia in guerra: Una conversazione fra storia e storiografia* (Rome, 1996), p. 102.

16 Michele Sarfatti, *Gli ebrei nell'Italia fascista: Vicende, identità, persecuzione* (Turin, 2000), p. 147.

17 For a summary of the legislation, see Sarfatti, *Gli ebrei nell'Italia fascista*, pp. 154–64.

10 The new community: women and youth

1 Married women represented only 5–6 per cent of the women in the civil service, as against 20 per cent of all working women who were married, so the impact of this legislation was limited. See Caplan, *Government without Administration*, p. 99.

2 On this point, see Tim Mason, *Social Policy in the Third Reich: The Working Class and the 'National Community'* (Providence and Oxford, 1993) and *Nazism, Fascism and the Working Class* (Jane Caplan (ed.)) (Cambridge, 1995). In contrast David Schoenbaum argued for a substantial alteration of class and social status under nazism. See *Hitler's Social Revolution* (New York, 1967)/ More convincing is Ian Kershaw's conclusion:

> The most continuous, and usually the most dominant, influence upon the subjective perceptions by differing social groups of their socio-economic position during the Third Reich was, it seems, formed by the material conditions that directly affected the everyday lives of the population. And here, inequalities, and

the persistent feelings of exploitation appear to have changed little in the period of the Dictatorship. The alienation of the working class, the massive disillusionment of discontent in most sections of the population deriving from their actual daily experience under Nazism is scarsely compatible with Schoenbaum's view that 'interpreted social reality . . . reflected a society united like no other in recent German history' and a status revolution amounting to a 'triumph of eqalitarianism'.

See Kershaw, *The Nazi Dictatorship: Problems and Perspectives of Interpretation* (3rd edn, London, 1993), p. 145.

3 Perry Willson, *Peasant Women and Politics in Fascist Italy: The Massaie Rurali* (London and New York, 2002), p. 87.

4 Claudia Koonz noted how the emancipated woman symbolized cultural crisis and degeneration for the Nazis. See *Mothers in the Fatherland: Women, the Family and Nazi Politics* (New York, 1987), pp. 98–9. The equation of female emancipation with natonal decline had been a staple in conservative thought since the nineteenth-century. See Susanna Barrows, *Distorting Mirrors: Visions of the Crowd in Late Nineteenth-Century France* (New Haven, 1981).

5 The Fascist organization for peasant women, the *Massaie rurali* grew to a membership of 3 million by the end of the regime. See Willson, *Peasant Women and Politics*, p. 2.

6 De Grazia, *How Fascism Ruled Women*, p. 155.

7 Konrad H. Jarausch, *The Unfree Professions: German Lawyers, Teachers and Engineers, 1900–1950* (Cambridge, MA, 1990), p. 157.

8 Claudia Koonz, *The Nazi Conscience* (Cambridge, MA, 2003), p. 136;

9 De Grazia, *How Fascism Ruled Women*, pp. 81–3.

10 In 1939 the *fasci femminili* had 774,181 members and grew by 1942 to little over one million. In contrast, the PNF ballooned from 2.6 million members in 1939 to 4.7 million in 1942. The Fascist umbrella youth organization expanded from roughly 7.9 million to almost 8.8 million. See Renzo De Felice, *Mussolini l'alleato*, part 1: *L'Italia in guerra 1940–1943*, p. 969.

11 Tracy Koon, *Believe, Obey, Fight: Political Socialization in Fascist Italy 1922–1943* (Chapel Hill, 1985), pp. 173–83.

12 Noakes and Pridham, *Nazism 1918–1945*, vol. 2, p. 433.

13 Noakes and Pridham, vol. 2, p. 443.

11 Culture and society

1 For an interesting analysis of these conflicts, see Mabel Berezin, *Making the Fascist Self: The Political Culture of Interwar Italy* (Ithaca, NY, 1997), p. 139.

2 Michael Burleigh, *The Third Reich: A New History* (New York, 2000), p. 264.

3 Gentile's emphasis on elite formation led him to accept the introduction of religious instruction for the masses in the elementary schools in his 1923 reform. However, this concession to the Catholic Church was also dictated by Mussolini's courtship of the Vatican.

4 On this theme, see the catalogue of the exhibition, *Les realismes* (Paris, 1981).

5 On the integration of cultural constituencies, see Alan E. Steinweis, *Art, Ideology, and Economics in Nazi Germany: The Reich Chambers of Music, Theater and the Visual Arts* (Chapel Hill and London, 1993), Chapter 4, 'Varieties of Patronage'. For Italy, see Marla Susan Stone, *The Patron State: Culture and Politics in Fascist Italy* (Princeton, 1998).

6 On the role of intellectuals during the Fascist years, especially during the 1930s and 1940s, see Ruth Ben-Ghiat, *Fascist Modernities: Italy, 1922–1945* (Berkeley, 2001).

7 The importance of the *Accademia d'Italia* can be seen in the list of its presidents: former foreign minister Tommaso Tittoni, Guglielmo Marconi (who also headed the National Research council), Gabriele D'Annunzio and former Interior minister Luigi Federzoni. Only one woman, the writer Ada Negri, was a member. On this process, see Gabriele Turi, *Lo Stato educatore*, pp. 104–5, 111–12.

8 On the integration of professions into the state, see Gabriele Turi, *Lo Stato educatore: Politica e intellettuali nell'Italia fascista* (Bari, 2002). Turi establishes the connection between professional regulation and its extension into racial policy.

9 Turi, *Lo Stato educatore*, p. 100.

10 On the creation and evolution of the Ministry of Popular Culture, see Philip V. Cannistraro, 'Burocrazia e politica culturale nello stato fascista', *Storia contemporanea*, I (June 1970), 273–98.

11 See Emilio Gentile, 'Impending Modernity: Fascism and the Ambivalent Image of the United States', *Journal of Contemporary History*, 28 (1993), 7–29. See also James Hay, *Popular Film in Fascist Italy: The Passing of the Rex* (Bloomington, Ill, 1987) and Marcia Landy, *Fascism in Film: The Italian Commercial Cinema, 1931–1943* (Princeton, 1986).

12 In contrast, the Nazi regime embarked after 1935 on a campaign to eliminate the theatrical productions of the Catholic Church. See Steinweis, *Art, Ideology and Economics in Nazi Germany,* p. 137.

13 On the blending of the various artistic schools in the 1932 Mostra, see Maria Stone, 'Staging Fascism: The Exhibition of the Fascist Revolution', *Journal of Contemporary History*, 28 (1993), 215–43.

14 See Michela Nacci, *L'antiamericanismo in Italia negli anni trenta* (Turin, 1989) for the connection between the anti-modernism of the 1930s and the image of American culture.

15 Note the work of Ruth Ben-Ghiat in note 2.

16 Jarausch, *Unfree Professions*, p. 105.

17 For an overview of the process by which the professions were co-opted, see Jarausch, *Unfree Professions*.
18 See the introduction of Stephanie Bartron to *Degenerate Art: The Fate of the Avant-Garde in Nazi Germany* (Los Angeles, 1991), p. 9.
19 See David Welch, *The Third Reich: Politics and Propaganda* (London, 1993), p. 28. Critics also needed a work permit to practise what was left of their profession.
20 For the brief Goebbels–Strauss honeymoon, see Steinweis, *Art, Ideology and Economics*, pp. 51–4.
21 On the Nolde case, see Russell A. Berman, 'German Primitivism/ Primitive Germany', in Richard J. Golsan (ed.), *Fascism, Aesthetics, and Culture* (Hanover and London, 1992), pp. 57–66.
22 Goebbels staked out very broad jurisdiction for his ministry and ran into trouble from the various state cultural ministries, from the Reich Education ministry that insisted on controlling its own civil servants in the art education establishment, and from the Labour Front that sought to protect its role in popular culture. See Steinweis, *Art, Ideology, and Economics*, pp. 63–8.

12 Consensus and coercion under fascism and nazism

1 For Nazi propaganda, the following are useful: Ian Kershaw, *Popular Opinion and Political Dissent in the Third Reich* (Oxford, 1983); David Welsh (ed.), *Nazi Propaganda: The Power and Limitations* (London, 1983); Z. A. B. Zeman, *Nazi Propaganda* (2nd edn, Oxford, 1973). For Italy see: Pier Giorgio Zunino, *L'ideologia del fascismo: Miti, credenze, e valori nella stabilizzazione del regime* (Bologna, 1985); Luisa Passerini, *Fascism in Popular Memory: The Cultural Experience of the Turin Working Class* (Cambridge, 1987); Victoria De Grazia, *The Culture of Consent* (New York, 1981; and Philip Cannistraro, *La Febbrica del consenso* (Bari, 1975)
2 Mimmo Franzinelli, *I tentacoli dell'Ovra: Agenti, collaboratori e vittime della polizia politica fascista* (Turin, 1999), p. 237. This work is an exhaustive study of the Italian polical police and the repressive apparatus. Also important is the article by Paul Corner, 'Italian Fascism: Whatever Happened to Dictatorship', *Journal of Modern History* 74 (2, June 2002), 325–57.
3 Enzo Collotti and Lutz Klinkhammer, *Il fascismo e l'Italia in guerra* (Rome, 1996), pp. 14–16.
4 Robert Gellately, 'Surveillance and Disobedience: Aspects of Political Policing in Nazi Germany', in Christian Leitz (ed.), *The Third Reich: The Essential Readings* (Oxford, 1999), pp. 187–9, 198; also Gellately, *The Gestapo and German Society: Enforcing Racial Policy, 1933–1945* (Oxford, 1990).

5 Curiously, reports in the Italian press indicate that ordinary Italians who visit Mussolini's tomb still leave requests and appeals as they might for traditional saints.

6 On this point, see Ian Kershaw, *The Hitler Myth: Image and Reality in the Third Reich* (Oxford, 1987), and Renzo De Felice, *Mussolini il fascista: Gli anni del consenso* (Turin, 1974).

7 On Hitler's popularity, see Ian Kershaw, *The Hitler Myth*. For the position of Mussolini, see Renzo De Felice, *Mussolini il duce: Gli anni del consenso 1929–1936*.

8 Fundamental on fascism's religious vision is George Mosse, *The Nationalization of the Masses: Political Symbolism and Mass Movements in Germany from the Napoleonic Wars through the Third Reich* (New York, 1975); see also Emilio Gentile, 'Fascism as Political Religion', *Journal of Contemporary History*, 25 (1990), 229–51. It might be that the parallel with religion merely obscures more than it clarifies and may be just a restatement of earlier analyses that stressed the role of myth in fascism and nazism. For an analysis of fascism as political religion, see Griffin, *The Nature of Fascism*, pp. 30–2.

13 The status of the military

1 Giorgio Rochat and Giulio Massobrio, *Breve storia dell'Esercito italiano dal 1861 al 1943* (Turin, 1978), p. 220.

2 MacGregor Knox, *Common Destiny: Dictatorship, Foreign Policy, and War in Fascist Italy and Nazi Germany* (Cambridge, 2000), p. 209.

3 Cited in Omer Bartov, *Hitler's Army: Soldiers, Nazis, and War in the Third Reich* (New York and Oxford, 1991), p. 129.

14 Imperialism and expansion: the Fascist and Nazi regimes and the challenge of war

1 Several recent studies have linked the ambitions of Hitler and Mussolini: MacGregor Knox, *Common Destiny* (Cambridge, 2000) and *Hitler's Italian Allies: Royal Armed Forces, Fascist Regime and the War of 1940–1943* (Cambridge, 2000); Aristotle Kallis, *Fascist Ideology: Territory and Expansionism in Italy and Germany, 1922–1945* (London and New York, 2000).

2 Hitler's foreign policy has been much more extensively covered than Mussolini's but the situation has been addressed by the publication of three new works: Reynolds M. Salerno, *Vital Crossroads: Mediterranean Origins of the Second World War, 1935–1940* (Ithaca, NY, 2002); R. Bruce Strang, *On the Fiery March: Mussolini Prepares for War* (Westport, CT, 2003); and Robert Mallett, *Mussolini and the Origins of the Second World War, 1933–1940* (Houndmills, 2003).

3 On Italy's preparation for war in 1940–1, see MacGregor Knox, *Mussolini Unleashed 1939–1941: Politics and Strategy in Fascist Italy's Last War* (London, 1982).

4 On the primacy of the political in Mussolini and his distrust of the military, see Renzo De Felice, *Mussolini l'alleato: L'Italia in guerra 1940–1943*, Part 1: p. 52.

5 On the two alternatives for German rearmament, see Berenice Carroll, *Design for Total War: Arms and Economics in the Third Reich* (The Hague, 1968), pp. 86–8.

6 Both Hitler and Mussolini held to their short war illusions until well after the war turned against them. Neither leader accepted full mobilization of the civilian economy until 1942. A reflection of this was Nazi Germany's reluctance to mobilize female labour. As late as 1944, Germany still had over 1 million female domestic servants, when Britain had practically eliminated that category. Milward also noted that the number of women working in 1943–4 was only 600,000 above the 1939 figure. See Alan Milward, *War, Economy and Society 1939–1945* (London, 1977), pp. 220–1.

7 The process has been traced in the classic study by F. W. Deakin, *The Brutal Friendship* (New York, 1966).

Conclusion

1 Kershaw, 'Working Toward the Führer: Reflections on the Nature of the Hitler Dictatorship', in Leitz, *The Third Reich*, p. 248.

2 On the Italian treatment of the Jews and the development of anti-Semitism, see Susan Zuccotti, *Italians and the Holocaust: Persecution, Rescue, and Survival* (New York, 1981) and *Under his Very Windows: The Vatican and the Holocaust in Italy* (New Haven, 2000); David Kertzer, *The Popes against the Jews: The Vatican's Role in the Rise of Modern Anti-Semitism* (New York, 2001); Alexander Stille, *Betrayal: Five Jewish Families under Fascism* (New York, 1981). Joel Blatt pushed back the origins of anti-Semitism in 'The Battle of Turin, 1933–1936: Carlo Rosselli, Giustizia e Libertà, OVRA, and the Origins of Mussolini's Anti-Semitism Campaign', *Journal of Modern Italian Studies* I (1, 1995). On the differing reactions of Nazis and Fascists, see Jonathan Steinberg, *All or Nothing: The Axis and the Holocaust, 1941–1943* (London, 1990). On the general subject of Italian racial thinking, see Aaron Gillette, *Racial Theories in Fascist Italy* (London, 2002).

3 For a discussion of these continuities, see Norbert Frei, *Adenauer's Germany and the Nazi Past: The Politics of Amnesty and Integration*, forward by Fritz Stern (New York, 2002) and the survey of recent writing in Edith Raim, 'Coping with the Nazi Past: Germany and the Legacy of the Third Reich', *Contemporary European History* 12 (4, November 2003), 547–9.136

Index